Things Pertaining to Bodhi

THINGS PERTAINING TO BODHI

The Thirty-seven Aids to Enlightenment

CHAN MASTER
Sheng Yen

SHAMBHALA
Boston & London
2010

FRONTISPIECE: Master Sheng Yen (1930–2009)
writing the Chinese character for *Chan*.
*Photo provided by Dharma Drum Mountain Cultural
and Educational Foundation. Used by permission; all rights reserved.*

SHAMBHALA PUBLICATIONS, INC.
HORTICULTURAL HALL
300 MASSACHUSETTS AVENUE
BOSTON, MASSACHUSETTS 02115
www.shambhala.com

The author gratefully acknowledges permission to reprint
"The Last Admonition," from *The Maha Parinibbana Sutta*,
translated from the Pali by Sister Vajira and Francis Story
(Kandy, Sri Lanka, Buddhist Publication Society, 1998).

Printed in the United States of America
⊗ This edition is printed on acid-free paper that meets
the American National Standards Institute z39.48 Standard.
♻ Shambhala Publications makes every effort to print on recycled
paper. For more information please visit www.shambhala.com.
Distributed in the United States by Random House, Inc.,
and in Canada by Random House of Canada Ltd

LIBRARY OF CONGRESS CATALOGING-IN-PUBLICATION DATA
Shengyan, 1930–2009
Things pertaining to bodhi: the Thirty-seven aids to enlightenment /
Chan Master Sheng Yen. —1st ed.
p. cm.
Includes index.
"Dr. Rebecca Li's concurrent oral translation of Master Sheng Yen's
lectures, on which this book is based"—Introd.
ISBN 978-1-59030-790-8 (pbk.: alk. paper)
1. Enlightenment (Buddhism)—Requisites.
2. Spiritual life—Buddhism. I. Title.
BQ4399.S54 2010
294.3'4422—dc22
2010003327

Contents

Acknowledgments

TEACHER: Chan Master Sheng Yen

ORAL TRANSLATION: Dr. Rebecca Li

TRANSCRIPTION: Chang Wen Fashi, Bruce Rickenbacher, Sheila Sussman

EDITOR: Ernest Heau

PUBLICATIONS: Iris Wang

We join our palms in gratitude to Master Sheng Yen, who serenely crossed over to nirvana on February 3, 2009, in Taiwan.

Editor's Introduction

THE SUBJECT OF THIS BOOK is the body of teachings of the Buddha known in the Pali dialect as the *bodhipakkhiya*, and in Sanskrit as *bodhipakshika*. The term translates literally as "things pertaining to bodhi (enlightenment)," or the "factors of bodhi." The Chinese name for this body of teachings is *sanshiqi dao ping*, literally, "thirty-seven aspects of the way." However, the teachings have also been referred to as "the thirty-seven factors of enlightenment," or "the thirty-seven aids to enlightenment." The latter is the usage adopted in Dr. Rebecca Li's concurrent oral translation of Master Sheng Yen's lectures, on which this book is based. In his monumental book on the bodhipakkhiya, the Theravada monk Thanissaro Bhikkhu refers to the teachings as "wings to awakening."[1] The title we have given to Master Sheng Yen's treatment of the subject, *Things Pertaining to Bodhi,* was chosen for brevity as well as allegiance to the original term, bodhipakshika. In this introduction, for convenience and brevity, we will refer to the teachings as the bodhipakshika.

Between 1977 and 2006, it was Master Sheng Yen's practice to alternate between three-month stays at Dharma Drum Mountain, the monastery he founded in Jinshan, Taiwan, and the Chan Meditation

Center in Queens, New York. On Sunday afternoons between May 1999 and November 2003, when he was in New York, the Master gave freely of his energies to teach on the bodhipakshika. These lectures have been compiled and edited into this posthumous volume.

One of the first things to note about the bodhipakshika is that the teachings they comprise were not given by the Buddha in their totality at any one time or in any one sutra. Rather, the disparate but related teachings of the bodhipakshika were presented at different times in the Buddha's long career. In other words, there is no one locale during his life, or one particular scripture in the Buddhist canon, where all of the bodhipakshika were expounded in their fullness by the Buddha. For example, the seventh and last group in the bodhipakshika, the Noble Eightfold Path, comes directly out of the fourth noble truth from the Buddha's very first sermon, the *Dharmachakra-parvatana* (Turning of the Dharma Wheel) *Sutra*.

In another example, the Four Foundations of Mindfulness, which comprise the first group in the bodhipakshika, are contained in the *Satipatthana Sutra*, and were presented as a separate teaching, not as part of an inclusive set known as the bodhipakshika. In a real sense, therefore, the bodhipakshika can be considered an anthology, a collection, or gathering if you will, of the Buddha's teachings on how to traverse the path to enlightenment. Indeed, in *The Wings to Awakening* Thanissaro Bhikkhu treats them in the context of an anthology.

What Are the Bodhipakshika?

If the bodhipakshika were not presented as a distinct and unitary set of teachings, where do they come from? They come from the seven groups of practices that the Buddha expounded to his followers at different times and places, as paradigms of practice toward *bodhi*—enlightenment. Each of these seven groups breaks down into further practices or factors, bringing the total of these elements to thirty-seven. And as mentioned before, the seven groups of practices do not necessarily occur in sequence in the canon, although they are meant to be sequential in practice.

The number thirty-seven thus refers to the total number of factors contained overall in the seven groups of practices:

1. The Four Foundations of Mindfulness (*smriti-upasthana*)
2. The Four Proper Exertions (*samyak-prahanani*)
3. The Four Steps to Magical Powers (*riddhipada*)
4. The Five Roots (*indriya*)
5. The Five Powers (*bala*)
6. The Seven Factors of Enlightenment (*sapta-bodhyanga*)
7. The Noble Eightfold Path (*arya ashtangika-marga*)

References in the Abhidharma

One place where the bodhipakshika are referenced in their entirety is in the third section of the Tripitaka, the Abhidharma. Following is an abridged tabular representation, omitting details not relevant to this discussion, of where the bodhipakshika stand within the Tripitaka, the "three baskets" of the Buddhist canon—the Vinaya, the Sutras, and the Abhidharma.

THE TRIPITAKA

Vinaya Pitaka (Codes of conduct)

Sutra Pitaka (Sermons of the Buddha)

Abhidharma Pitaka (Seven books of treatises and philosophical analysis including the *Vibhanga*)

Vibhanga (subdivided into eighteen books)

BOOK 5: Five Roots and Five Powers (comprising two groups)

BOOK 7: Four Foundations of Mindfulness

BOOK 8: Four Proper Exertions

BOOK 9: Four Steps to Magical Powers

BOOK 10: Seven Factors of Enlightenment

BOOK 11: Noble Eightfold Path

The Role of the Bodhipakshika in Enlightenment

To say that the bodhipakshika together constitute a road map to enlightenment would be convenient and also correct Buddhadharma, since the Buddha himself admonished his followers to engage these practices. If misunderstood, however, this could be a restricting and limiting view. Another way to think of it is to ask: the bodhipakshika may be sufficient in terms of reaching enlightenment, but are they necessary? From the point of view of Chan Buddhism, it would seem at first sight that they are not necessary, since most of the great Chan masters did not spend much time teaching the bodhipakshika as a path to enlightenment. What they did teach were the direct methods of Chan, primarily the method of *gong'an* (J., koan) and the method of Silent Illumination (J., *shikantaza*). So is there a discontinuity between the Buddha's teaching of the bodhipakshika and the teachings of the Chan and Zen masters? Master Sheng Yen deals with this conundrum to a significant degree in this book, but without addressing it as a conundrum. However, one could say that Master Sheng Yen's lectures go some distance toward reconciling the seeming discrepancy between the incremental path of the bodhipakshika and the sudden enlightenment of the Chan and Zen masters.

Master Sheng Yen sees the difference partly as a matter of individual disposition: "Since most Chan masters teach sudden enlightenment, they do not talk much about the Thirty-seven Aids, which are considered gradual methods. However, I do teach gradual methods as the foundation for practice toward sudden enlightenment. For those capable of realizing sudden enlightenment, that is wonderful and they can dispense with the gradual methods. However, those for whom sudden enlightenment is not that feasible can practice gradual methods as a foundation for the sudden methods."

Also he says: "We often associate Chan with sudden enlightenment, but Chan practice does indeed progress in stages. However, one does not take each stage as an ultimate goal. Therefore, even though Chan speaks of sudden enlightenment, it also embraces the gradualism implied in the Thirty-seven Aids."

In his lectures, perhaps the praxis that Master Sheng Yen most often returns to in order to reconcile the gradualism of the bodhipakshika and the directness of the Mahayana is the need for *samadhi*—meditative concentration—in order to cultivate wisdom. In other words, whether one follows the gradual path of the bodhipakshika or the sudden path of Chan, samadhi is a necessary ingredient for realizing wisdom.

In addition to samadhi, Master Sheng Yen sees the need to cultivate virtue as another key for progress on the path. In fact, the need for both samadhi and virtue is constant and crucial, whether one practices the gradualism of the bodhipakshika or the sudden illumination of Chan. And how does one cultivate virtue? Precisely by practicing the second group from the bodhipakshika, the Four Proper Exertions: "To keep unwholesome states not yet arisen from arising, to cease unwholesome states already arisen, to give rise to wholesome states not yet arisen, and to continue wholesome states already arisen."

Finally, to cap a point already made implicitly, one should not see samadhi and virtue as separate practices but as two sides of the same coin: a virtuous life empowers samadhi, and samadhi enhances a virtuous life.

If one sees practice this way, then any formal differences between gradualism and sudden enlightenment do not seem that important.

It could also be misleading if one takes the bodhipakshika as reducible to a sequential and linear regimen toward enlightenment, always and without deviation, putting one foot in front of the other. Thanissaro Bhikkhu, using a very modern metaphor, has suggested that the bodhipakshika can be seen as a hologram. Put simply, this would mean that any one of the thirty-seven factors reflects, and in some sense contains, all the others. Although Master Sheng Yen does not use this term, the holographic view also resonates in his teaching that in the Mahayana approach, direct contemplation of the mind and its activities cuts across or penetrates the disparate groups and factors of the bodhipakshika. This may be considered a *spatial* view of the bodhipakshika.

One can also take a *temporal* view of the bodhipakshika. For example, as soon as one begins in a real sense to practice the Four Foundations of Mindfulness, which are the first group in the sequence, one is also already practicing the last of the Noble Eightfold Path, Right Concentration, or meditation. In other words, all seven groups in the bodhipakshika can be seen as coterminous from the point of view of the practitioner, depending on his or her state of attainment. When perfect enlightenment is realized, the whole of the bodhipakshika is also realized. It is not as if, in beginning with the first foundation of mindfulness, the eighth noble path lies somewhere in the distant and sequential future. Rather, from the point of view of praxis it is here and now. In this sense, when you practice one of the factors, you practice all of them. And yet, the nature of the practices is such that when one finally arrives at them, they have not lost their individuality or their cogency. One still needs to go through them to complete the course of enlightenment; the arhat-to-be should traverse the whole bodhipakshika. In other words, to borrow a mathematical term, coursing through the practice of the bodhipakshika can be somewhat of a recursive experience. One begins anew at each step, but by the same token, when one arrives one realizes that in some real sense one has already been there. But the scenery and the context have changed, widened, and deepened beyond measure. Perhaps what we are saying is that there is no shortcut to enlightenment, but at the same time, enlightenment is accessible from any point of the practice, at any time when the mind is ripe and ready to receive it. In this view, seeing the bodhipakshika as sequential is not necessarily inconsistent with seeing them as simultaneous, existing all at once, and vice versa.

So if one begins with mindfulness of breath, does this mean that one is also practicing, for example, the first step to magical powers, *chandra*, which Master Sheng Yen describes as the "will to attain the wondrous and supreme *dhyana* where wisdom manifests"? In truth, the answer to this question can only be found in the mind of the individual practitioner, if and when they arrive at that point. And perhaps in realizing this, we come closer to understanding the wonder and the mystery of the bodhipakshika, the Thirty-seven Aids to Enlightenment.

The Buddha's Parinirvana

Perhaps there is no better way to illustrate the importance of the bodhipakshika than to recall the Buddha's Last Admonition to the assembly prior to entering parinirvana, from the *Mahaparinirvana Sutra*. Here he speaks to Ananda, the disciple on whom he relied to remember and disseminate his teachings. And so three months prior to crossing over to nirvana, the Buddha said these words:

THE LAST ADMONITION

"So, then, Ananda, let us go to the hall of the Gabled House, in the Great Forest." And the Venerable Ananda replied: "So be it, Lord."

Then the Blessed One, with the Venerable Ananda, went to the hall of the Gabled House, in the Great Forest. And there he spoke to the Venerable Ananda, saying: "Go now, Ananda, and assemble in the hall of audience all the bhikkhus who dwell in the neighborhood of Vesali."

"So be it, Lord." And the Venerable Ananda gathered all the bhikkhus who dwelt in the neighborhood of Vesali, and assembled them in the hall of audience. And then, respectfully saluting the Blessed One, and standing at one side, he said: "The community of bhikkhus is assembled, Lord. Now let the Blessed One do as he wishes."

Thereupon the Blessed One entered the hall of audience, and taking the seat prepared for him, he exhorted the bhikkhus, saying: "Now, O bhikkhus, I say to you that these teachings of which I have direct knowledge and which I have made known to you—these you should thoroughly learn, cultivate, develop, and frequently practice, that the life of purity may be established and may long endure, for the welfare and happiness of the multitude, out of compassion for the world, for the benefit, well-being, and happiness of gods and men.

"And what, bhikkhus, are these teachings? They are the four foundations of mindfulness, the four right efforts, the four constituents of psychic power, the five faculties, the five powers, the seven factors of enlightenment, and the Noble Eightfold Path. These, bhikkhus, are the teachings of which I have direct knowledge, which I have made known to you, and which you should thoroughly learn, cultivate, develop, and frequently practice, that the life of purity may be established and may long endure, for the welfare and happiness of the multitude, out of compassion for the world, for the benefit, well-being, and happiness of gods and men."

Then the Blessed One said to the bhikkhus: "So, bhikkhus, I exhort you: All compounded things are subject to vanish. Strive with earnestness. The time of the Tathagata's Parinibbana is near. Three months hence the Tathagata will utterly pass away."

And having spoken these words, the Happy One, the Master, spoke again, saying:

> My years are now full ripe, the life span left is short.
> Departing, I go hence from you, relying on myself
>   alone.
> Be earnest, then, O bhikkhus, be mindful and of
>   virtue pure!
> With firm resolve, guard your own mind!
> Whoso untiringly pursues the Dhamma and the
>   Discipline
> Shall go beyond the round of births and make an end
>   of suffering.[2]

To close this introduction, it would be appropriate to quote Master Sheng Yen's final teaching before he passed over to nirvana on February 3, 2009, in Taiwan:

> *Busy with nothing, growing old.*
> *Within emptiness, weeping, laughing.*
> *Intrinsically, there is no "I."*
> *Life and death, thus cast aside.*

—ERNEST HEAU

NOTES

1. Thanissaro Bhikkhu, *The Wings to Awakening: An Anthology from the Pali Canon* (Barre, Mass.: Dhamma Dana Publications 1996), www.dharma.org/bcbs/Pages/documents/wings.pdf.

2. Excerpted from part 3 of the translation from the Pali of the *Maha Parinibbana Sutta* by Sister Vajira and Francis Story: *Last Days of the Buddha: The Maha Parinibbana Sutta* (Kandy, Sri Lanka: Buddhist Publication Society, 1998). Reprinted with permission.

1

THE FOUR FOUNDATIONS
OF MINDFULNESS

THE FOUR FOUNDATIONS of Mindfulness are practices that help us to cultivate samadhi in order to generate wisdom. Through samadhi and wisdom we realize the true nature of phenomena and the emptiness of the self. Thus, samadhi and wisdom are the liberation paths to enlightenment. So although practicing samadhi is not the goal of the Four Foundations, it goes hand in hand with the goal, which is wisdom.

As preparation for the Four Foundations, one should practice the Five Methods of Stilling the Mind. The reason is that in order to effectively practice the Four Foundations, one's mind should be sufficiently calm and collected. The Five Methods of Stilling the Mind are preliminary methods that help us to detach from wandering thoughts, to quiet the chatter of the mind, and to bring it to the one-pointed state. Having achieved samadhi, we can contemplate the Four Foundations and thus generate wisdom.

The Five Methods of Stilling the Mind are (1) contemplating the breath, (2) contemplating the impurity of the body, (3) contemplating loving-kindness, (4) contemplating causes and conditions, and (5) contemplating the limits of phenomena, or contemplating the name of a buddha (depending on the tradition).

It is difficult to calm a mind that is vexed and full of wandering thoughts. At such times it is very useful to begin with the first and simplest method: counting or observing the breath. Some schools start with contemplating impurity, others practice loving-kindness. Methods such as contemplating causes and conditions and contemplating the limits of phenomena are less common. Pure Land practitioners will recite Amitabha Buddha's name (Chin., Amitofo) to attain the same result, but one may also recite any buddha's name. One may also recite the name of Avalokiteshvara Bodhisattva (Chin., Guanyin Pusa). These are all methods for calming the mind.

It is not our purpose here to go into detail on the Five Methods because they lie outside the framework of the Thirty-seven Aids, except to note their importance to practicing the Four Foundations of Mindfulness. After one has been practicing the Five Methods and one's mind has calmed, one should begin to practice the Four Foundations, starting with mindfulness of the body.

The Four Foundations of Mindfulness are methods of contemplation to attain mindfulness of the body, including its impurities; mindfulness of sensations as sources of suffering; mindfulness of the transient nature of thoughts; and mindfulness of the emptiness of phenomena, or dharmas. Therefore, to practice the Four Foundations is to deal directly with the vexations we constantly generate within us.

We are complacent when things are going well and think it is not so difficult to avoid suffering. When we are warm and comfortable, well fed and rested, it is easy to feel there is little suffering in the body. When our mind is at ease, without much worry in our daily life, we tend to think that we don't need diligent practice to maintain that ease. However, it is impossible to predict when sickness or injury will come, or when something will disturb our mind. When these things happen, it is not easy to just put them aside. We often end up seeing a doctor to heal our body, or a therapist to heal our emotions.

A correct method of practice will help us to feel ease of mind and body regardless of circumstances. Whichever method we use, the main principle is to always relax the body and the mind. This way we can greatly reduce both our physical suffering and mental burdens.

Mindfulness of the Body

All our problems come from the interactions and conflicts between our body, our mind, and the environment. Of these, the mind is most important because it senses the body and experiences the environment. Body, mind, and environment together make up our sense of self. We think this is "my body" and "my environment." Who has these ideas? It is "I," the sense of self. You may well think your body is "you," but if I ask you if your body is the environment, you will probably say no. Common sense says that your body is "you" and the environment is not. So when there is opposition between the body and the environment, who suffers? It is "you" who suffers. It is very normal to feel this way.

Some may not think that they are in conflict with their body, but everyone has experienced times when their body and mind are at odds. Again, is your body yourself? If your body is yourself, then isn't it odd that your body and your mind should be in contradiction? From that, one can reason that your body is probably not your self. You may think, "Of course the body and the mind are in conflict sometimes, but surely my mind is my self." But is your mind really your self? Have you never experienced one thought conflicting with the next thought? What about conflicts between the thoughts you have today and the thoughts you had yesterday? How about contradictions between your rational mind and your emotions? Only a fool would say they never have contradictory thoughts.

Our sense of ego can be small or large. When our ego is very inflated, we will think of the body as our self and even take the environment as our self. As a result we are confused and want to control our body *and* the environment. Having to drag your body around is already a burden; how much greater a burden is it to carry the environment?

A disciple complained, "Shifu, I'm a person of very low status and people don't listen to me. I feel that I don't have any freedom. When I ask people for help, they ignore me. I suffer a lot from this."

I told him, "Well, even though you are a small person, your ego is so inflated that you include the environment as yourself and want to control it. You are foolish for not understanding your own limitations."

Because we identify the body as our self, and because the body interacts with the environment, we also tend to make the environment a part of our self-identity. This creates vexations. One of the sutras says, "Among all attachments that cause vexations, attachment to the body is the most difficult to give up." We create vexations within our mind, and then we take what happens in the environment and create more vexations. That is why the very first contemplation in the Four Foundations of Mindfulness is to contemplate the body.

We cherish our body and expect it to bring us happiness. We look to our sense organs as a source of pleasure. However, along with happiness and pleasure, the body brings us problems; it is not always as precious or as lovable as we like to think. The fact is that the body is impure. I am not referring to sweating and smelling bad; I am talking about the problems that the body generates for our mind. Some obvious examples are when the body feels discomfort, when it is tired, sick, hungry, and so on. All of these are sufferings caused by the body.

Most of all, the body causes vexations for the mind. When the body conflicts with the environment, when it is out of balance with the world, then that creates vexations in our mind. If the body were pure, it would bring us only joy and wisdom. Since it does not do that, we can conclude that the body is impure. Ultimately, what makes the body impure is our sense of self. Instead of looking at the body as a source of happiness, if we use it to practice, to connect with other people, it can then become a source of wisdom and merit. In this case, the body would be pure.

From the moment we are conceived, our body is subject to the impurities of physiology. The other day I had a blood test and my doctor talked about toxins in my blood. He said, "Everyone has toxins in their blood. No one's blood is totally free from toxins and plaque, unwanted particles and elements." He wasn't a Buddhist, but when I reflected on what he said, I agreed with him that the physical body is contaminated with all sorts of impurities. When a fundamental constituent of the body such as the blood is impure, that directly or indirectly leads to the suffering of illness and aging. Our mind is also contaminated by its resistance to the nature of suffering, and by our inability to accept it. Contrarily, if we contemplate that our sensations have a high potential for creating suffering, we will not be so excited when we experience pleasure, or grief stricken when we experience difficulties. This is because we are already armed with the knowledge and understanding that sensation is suffering and that existence is anguish. Not giving rise to vexation when we confront difficulty is itself wisdom. So when we can contemplate sensations as suffering, we will have wisdom, which relieves us from mental afflictions.

The important thing is to be aware of our body and its sensations. Please note that this is not the same as being attached to our body and our sensations. For instance, on a meditation retreat, we can accept and enjoy any bodily sensations of comfort and ease, without attaching to them or wanting them to continue. That way we will understand the sensations we experience instead of letting them generate worry and anxiety. Even though we understand that the body is impure, it is important to pay attention to it. When we are hungry, we eat; when we need a shower, we take a shower; when we are sick, we take medicine. We need to take care of the body so we can use it for practice.

Mindfulness of Sensations

When we contemplate our sensations, we are less likely to experience so much suffering. For instance, when someone is nice to you, you may feel happy at the time. If you then worry whether next time they will still be nice to you, you are now suffering. In that case, your nice sensation of happiness disappeared quickly. On the other hand, if someone insults you and you feel resentment, you are just adding more suffering for yourself. If we learn to contemplate our sensations and feelings, we will see them as transient phenomena and suffer less.

A kind of suffering that is related to sensation is bliss, which can be understood as happiness that arises from desire. In Buddhist cosmology there are three realms of existence (*triloka*) within the cycle of life and death (samsara). They are desire, form, and formlessness. The bliss that ordinary human beings mostly experience exists in the desire realm, which is the realm we live in. This bliss is coarser than the bliss of the form and formless realms, and it arises from the activities of the sense faculties, including the mind.

The form realm is the realm of samadhi, and in it one can experience different levels of meditative absorption and therefore different levels of bliss. The bliss of the form realm is subtler than the bliss of the desire realm because the activities of the sense faculties have greatly subsided. The bliss of the formless realm is the subtlest of all. Beings in this realm are pure spirits; therefore they have no sense faculties and because of that, do not experience desire. The bliss of the formless realm is not sensation per se but an approximation of liberation. It is approximate because beings in this realm still have a sense of self. Therefore, they are not yet really fully liberated from the cycle of death and rebirth. Nevertheless, the individual has been liberated from the limitations of body and mind. So corresponding to the realm, bliss ranges from the coarsest level of the desire realm, to the higher and subtler bliss of samadhi, and to the highest and subtlest of all, the bliss of the formless realm.

I believe you all have eaten lunch here today. Was it good? When you are hungry, any food is delicious; when you're not hungry, nothing tastes good. The pleasure of eating and drinking is mostly limited to the moments we are actually eating. The bliss in this circumstance is very brief, and then we need to do it again a few hours later. It is a pleasure to hear good music, but would hearing the same song over and over still be pleasurable? Or if you want to go to bed, you might find music disturbing.

Let's talk about tactile sensations. It feels very good to relieve an itch by scratching, doesn't it? How long does this pleasure last? If you go against nature and continue to scratch, the momentary pleasure may lead to pain. The pleasures associated with our sense faculties are momentary and transient.

Is there happiness in our lives? Some may say that they indeed have had happiness. For example, for most people their happiest time is when they are falling in love. Usually they do not realize that falling in love is also suffering. Consider the popular image of love as Cupid shooting an arrow through the hearts of the lovers. Doesn't this image convey the idea that love is also suffering? If they marry, the couple may strive to prolong that first feeling of love, but later on that may turn into a feeling of being stuck with each other.

It may be our natural desire to seek happiness and avoid suffering, yet we need doctors, hospitals, police, law courts, funeral homes, and so on. If the nature of existence is not suffering, why do countries need armies? Why do countries need protection from each other? Why do we need to go through customs when we travel? No sentient being can escape the reality of impermanence: it inflicts our lives with suffering, and it is intimately tied to the nature of suffering. Existence itself is the nature of suffering, and the more we try to resist suffering, the more we suffer.

The bliss of samadhi can be profound and vast, yet those who attain it are still in the realm of impermanence. Sooner or later their samadhi power will be exhausted, and they will return to an ordinary state. When they do, their bliss also vanishes. So even in the bliss of samadhi, we encounter the reality of impermanence.

These examples illustrate the meaning of the suffering of impermanence. However, understanding the pervasiveness of suffering in the midst of happiness and bliss does not mean we should fall into pessimism, hopelessness, and self-pity. On the contrary, if practitioners can profoundly contemplate the nature of suffering, they will be more able to face and accept suffering, and that will gradually release them from suffering. So this contemplation of sensations as suffering is a practice to relieve suffering and also to generate wisdom.

Mindfulness of the Mind

The third foundation of mindfulness is to contemplate the impermanence of mental states. The Buddhist psychology of the mind has three main aspects. The first is consciousness that arises through the sense faculties interacting with the external environment. Through the faculty of sight, we see things; through the faculty of hearing we hear things; and so on. All these mental phenomena are kinds of cognitive consciousness. The second aspect of the mind is reflection, which is the mind itself thinking and reflecting in isolation from sensations. This also occurs in sleep, where the mind can dream without relying on the sense faculties. The third aspect of the mind is the underlying substratum of consciousness that continues from one life to the next; it links the previous life to the present one, and will continue to exist in future lives.

With regard to contemplating the mind as impermanent, the first level of sensation is the coarsest and most easily perceived as transient. As one makes progress in mindfulness practice, the mind becomes increasingly subtle in its perceptions. One then becomes aware of the second level, where the mind reflects on its own phenomena, independent of the sense faculties. One becomes keenly aware of the transient nature of one's thoughts in isolation from the environment, the way they just rise and fall, and the mindfulness of that happening. The third and most subtle level of the mind also arises in meditation, where the mind is refined to the point where it can perceive countless past lives and countless future lives. The mind is also aware of itself becoming clearer and clearer. When we can personally experience this ongoing, impermanent nature of our own mind, that itself is wisdom, and with wisdom we are liberated from suffering. This is the purpose of contemplating the mind as impermanent.

In what way is it liberation to experience the impermanence of one's mind? Why is that wisdom? We ordinarily identify the mind as "my" mind, the body as "my" body. When you have a haircut, the hair that ends up on the floor, is that "you"? After you take a bath, what's left in the bathwater, is that "you"? You may not so willingly admit that these things are you, but they come from your body. Common sense says that we don't identify these things as "me." Well, then who are you? Some people may think, "I am my mind," and this is the crux of contemplating the mind as impermanent. Mind is "me" as a sense of self. Identifying the thinking process as oneself is the source of vexations and suffering. For example, when we identify with the thought of arrogance, this leads to suffering. When we identify with the feelings of jealousy and hatred, these mental states will lead to suffering.

When we examine our thoughts very closely, we see that we are taking those mental states as evidence of a permanent self. We believe that there is an "I" behind arrogance, hatred, jealousy, and so on. It is the constant self-referencing, the very subtle identifying of the mind with a sense of self, that is the source of suffering. When someone truly understands and perceives that the mind is constantly in flux, that it is just a mirror of impermanence, then one will stop seeing the thought-stream as the self, and suffering will not follow.

You may think, "Oh, this is a very lofty practice, a very high attainment." That is not necessarily so. One does not need to engage in deep samadhi to attain this. The real question is how to integrate this idea into our attitudes, and do that wherever we are and whenever we can. If in our life we can be mindful of our thinking process and become familiar with the idea of observing impermanence, we will gradually lessen our identification of these thoughts as "me," "mine," or "I." The more profound our understanding, the more profound our experience of what "no-self" means. And this reality of selflessness is wisdom, and that is freedom from suffering.

Understanding impermanence need not mean seeing life as dreadful. On the contrary, if we do not end our vexations and do not give rise to genuine insight and wisdom, then indeed one's suffering can seem very real and very permanent. Buddhist practitioners who contemplate the impurity of the body and contemplate impermanence will not be pessimistic. Rather, they will very actively engage in practice in order to sever vexations and give rise to insight and wisdom. Only then will one be released from suffering.

This means using one's body to help others while benefiting oneself; this also means using the mind to contemplate, to benefit self and others, and to embrace wholesome attitudes and views. This is Buddhist practice. When we actively engage our body and mind in a wholesome way, treading the path of Dharma, then and only then will one actualize impermanence and experience the nature of emptiness and selflessness. However, while realizing emptiness is liberation for oneself, other sentient beings still need help in liberating themselves. At that stage, one can wholeheartedly use one's body and mind to benefit others.

Mindfulness of Dharmas

The fourth foundation is mindfulness of dharmas. "Dharma" in Buddhism can be understood in two ways. The first meaning refers to all mental as well as physical phenomena. (By convention, we use a lower case when we have this meaning in mind.) The second meaning of "Dharma" refers to the teachings of the Buddha. But mindfulness of dharmas as selfless refers to the first type of dharma, that is, phenomena. To be more specific, we do not mean just material phenomena, but the phenomena of mind itself—mental events, mental processes, thought objects.

In Buddhism, thoughts are considered objects that exist in the mind. Some of the more detailed writings of the Yogachara (Mind-Only) school exhibit a comprehensive understanding of mind, dividing all mental states into dharmas, that is to say, things, events, and objects, giving detailed elaborations of them. The Abhidharma, the vast collection of early Buddhist treatises, also divides existence into dharmas, with similiarly detailed explanations.

Being mindful of dharmas means being aware of not only dharmas arising in our mind, but also how they cause affliction. This is because dharmas and their afflictions are constituents of our sense of self. When we can see that our sense of self comes from these negative mental states, then we are practicing mindfulness of dharmas. The Abhidharma and other texts go into elaborate detail on the different types of dharmas, but for the sake of simplicity, I want to just talk about dharmas with outflows and dharmas without outflows.

Whether they be physical or mental in origin, dharmas that are conditioned by phenomena are subject to change, deterioration, and impermanence. The arising of these dharmas in the ordinary mind results in suffering, or vexation. We call these dharmas with outflows. On the other hand, dharmas without outflows are not subject to causes and conditions. These dharmas arise in the mind of wisdom and are liberating. You can also call this the realization of selflessness.

Ordinary sentient beings only relate to dharmas with outflows, because this is a fact of existence: the way we think, the way we reflect on things, what we experience. All the objects of our experiences are subject to deterioration, change, and impermanence. Because they are conditioned, everything we experience constitutes dharmas with outflows.

You may have seen people who are laughing one minute and crying the next. Children are often like this, and so are people on meditation retreats. One time I brought a box of chocolates to some people I was visiting. The little girl in the family was very happy, thinking the chocolates were for her. When I told her it was for the whole family, the next instant she was crying. Can adults be like this too? Yes, we can.

So which mind is the "you," the happy one or the sad one? If "you" are the happy one, how come "you" are sometimes sad? If "you" is a permanent entity and it is sad, why is it sometimes happy? In fact, our sense of self constantly changes according to our mental states. There is no permanent, abiding self anywhere to be found. By examining the workings of our mind, we can understand that all phenomena are without a permanent, abiding self. By examining our daily experience, we will understand that all dharmas are conditional and transient, lacking fixed identity. We can also understand the workings of the mind through mindfulness of the body, mindfulness of sensations, and mindfulness of mind. This is the meaning of realizing the selflessness of dharmas. The point is to integrate these four kinds of contemplation into your daily life.

Student: When we contemplate impermanence, do we use our intellect, or just our awareness?

Sheng Yen: Really understanding impermanence is not intellectual; it is experiential. It is not something to ponder; it is something to be known. If you try to understand impermanence intellectually, you are more likely to get tired before any true wisdom arises. Impermanence is something one must personally experience. For example, in the immediacy of feeling pain, you know and you experience it. This is different from thinking, "OK, this pain is impermanent; it will go away." It's a process of filtering the experience of pain through understanding its impermanence. This involves cognition, but it is not thinking, "This pain will go away." It is rather understanding with your whole being that the reality you are experiencing is fundamentally impermanent.

Mahayana Approach to Contemplating Emptiness

We can practice the Four Foundations to cultivate mindfulness of the body, of sensations, of thoughts, and of dharmas. When we see that these factors are impermanent and result from causes and conditions coming together, we see that they have no enduring self-nature. Therefore we gain some wisdom.

Opposing the Four Foundations are the four upside-down views: attaching to our body; mistaking pleasure for happiness; taking thoughts of the mind as the self; and seeing phenomena as real. These are obstructions to liberation. The Four Foundations help us correct these upside-down views by reducing our vexations, allowing us to make progress toward wisdom. When we see that the body is really impure, we will not be so attached to it; when we see that sense pleasures ultimately bring suffering, we will not be so full of desire; when we see the mind as a collection of passing thoughts, we won't see the self as permanent; when we see that phenomena are without self, we will not be so attached to gain and loss.

In the Mahayana path we can accomplish the wisdom of the Four Foundations by contemplating emptiness directly. This idea comes from the *Mahaparinirvana Sutra*, which speaks of contemplating body, sensations, mind, and dharmas as empty. Through this contemplation we can realize wisdom. At first glance, this approach may seem easy, but unless one diligently practices the Four Proper Exertions (see chapter 2), it is very difficult.

How does one directly contemplate emptiness? Concerning the body, one sees that both the nature and the form of our body rise out of causes and conditions. And since they rise out of causes and conditions, they lack permanence; and lacking permanence, they are therefore empty of an abiding self. When we see that, we give rise to wisdom.

Sensations result from sense organs encountering sense objects; otherwise there would be no sensations. One sees that sensations do not reside *inside* our body, which only contains our sense organs. Neither do sensations reside *outside* our body, because outside our body are just the sense objects. But can we say that sensations must be somewhere in the *middle* where sense organs and sense objects come together? That makes no sense. So when we see that sensations reside neither inside our body, nor outside our body, nor in the middle, we can directly perceive that they are empty and give rise to wisdom.

This may sound like tricky reasoning, but it also explains how phenomena arise from causes and conditions. Sensations occur when sense organs and sense objects come together. Without these causes and conditions coming together, there would be no sensations. So if one can directly contemplate the arising of causes and conditions and how that brings about phenomena, then one is seeing emptiness.

Let's consider contemplating the mind. We give names like "greed," "hatred," "happiness," "jealousy," and "suspicion" to our thoughts and emotions. But these are just names, not the true nature of the workings of the mind. How can they have any fixed meaning if the mind is constantly in flux? If the mind has enduring reality, how can we be happy now and sad later, or vice versa? If emotions are real, how can we love something one instant and dis-like it the next? Precisely because the mind is constantly in motion, we cannot apply any name to it and say, "*This* is the mind." So the third contemplation is seeing that although we give names to thoughts and feelings, the names are not the mind itself.

How about contemplating the emptiness of phenomena? Once in Taiwan, a Chan master lectured on the emptiness of phenomena. Afterward a layperson walked up with a red envelope full of offer-ings for the lecturer. At this moment another Chan master in the audience came up and grabbed the envelope. The startled lecturer said, "But those offerings are for me!" The master from the audi-ence said, "You just said everything is empty. Money is empty; you are empty; I am empty. What difference does it make who gets the envelope?" He then handed the envelope to the lecturer and said, "Of course the offering belongs to you. The point I am making is, we talk about emptiness but how do we really practice it? How can we really see that everything is empty?"

It is not easy to see things like money, love, and relationships as empty. Can you think of your spouse, your boyfriend, or your girlfriend as empty? To begin seeing things as empty, diligently practice contemplation. In the meantime, keep reminding your-self to put aside greed and not attach to things like love, relation-ships, and money. Remind yourself that all things are ultimately empty.

When I was in Japan, a young scholar gave an excellent lecture on emptiness. Afterward we got together for lunch. We compli-mented this scholar on his talk, but said he should not eat because the food was empty anyway. He said, "Well, let's see. When empti-ness meets emptiness, isn't that also emptiness?" We agreed. Then he said, "Well, it should be all right for this empty food to go into my empty stomach." Everybody agreed, so we let him eat his lunch. [*Laughter*]

Does this direct approach to contemplation sound easy? Instead of contemplating the Four Foundations, can we just look at phenomena and say, "Oh, this is empty, that is empty"? No, it is not that easy. We need to practice with diligence before we can do that. That will be the topic of the Four Proper Exertions, the next group in the Thirty-seven Aids to Enlightenment.

2

THE FOUR PROPER EXERTIONS

THE CORRECT ORDER through the Thirty-seven Aids is to begin with the Four Foundations of Mindfulness to calm the mind, and then to practice the Four Proper Exertions to cultivate diligence. The Four Proper Exertions are thus the right attitudes for those on the Buddhist path. Without them one can become lax or even give up practicing entirely. How do the Four Proper Exertions relate to the Four Foundations of Mindfulness? Remember that we should first practice the Five Methods of Stilling the Mind to bring the mind to a one-pointed state. At that stage one can at most experience samadhi. After practicing the full course of the Four Foundations together with samadhi, wisdom can then arise. One is then on the path to liberation.

Another name for the Four Proper Exertions is the Four Cutting-offs of the Mind. By constantly reminding ourselves to practice, we cut off the thoughts that cause vexation. A third name is the Four Correct Ways of Cutting Off, pointing to the need to avoid mental sloth. A fourth name, the Four Kinds of Correct and Proper Excellence, encourages us to practice benevolence and stop bad deeds of body, speech, and mind. Without the diligence of the

Four Proper Exertions, one may falter in practice and give rise to the five hindrances of desire, anger, sloth, restlessness, and doubt.

What then are the Four Proper Exertions? They are (1) to keep unwholesome states not yet arisen from arising, (2) to cease unwholesome states already arisen, (3) to give rise to wholesome states not yet arisen, and (4) to continue wholesome states already arisen.

Buddhadharma really is about giving rise to wholesome states and stopping unwholesome states. What are wholesome and unwholesome states? The wholesome states are the ten virtues and the unwholesome states are their opposites—the ten nonvirtues. These ten virtues serve as the foundation of both the Hinayana and Mahayana paths. In fact, the ten virtues also reflect the moral standards for people in the lay life.

The Ten Virtues

The ten virtues are in three parts that correspond to actions, speech, and mind. The virtues relating to actions are refraining from killing, refraining from stealing, and refraining from sexual misconduct. The virtues relating to speech are refraining from lying, refraining from slandering, refraining from gossiping, and refraining from divisive speech. The virtues relating to the mind are cutting off greed, cutting off hatred, and cutting off ignorance. These ten virtues are the wholesome states that are cultivated by practicing the Four Proper Exertions. By contrast, the unwholesome states are the opposite of the ten virtues.

Dividing the ten virtues into three categories of actions, speech, and mind is just a coarse definition. If we leave out acts of the body and speech and just look at the mind, the scriptures talk about twenty kinds of unwholesome states of the mind, and eleven ways in which the mind can be wholesome. People may mistakenly believe that if they do not overtly do unwholesome things, they are in fact wholesome. But it is really in the mind where wholesomeness is cultivated, and only when the mind is free from vexation are we truly wholesome.

Wholesome and Unwholesome States

How can we distinguish between wholesome and unwholesome? We have already taken the view of wholesomeness as the ten virtues, and unwholesomeness as their opposites. We can also view wholesome and unwholesome states in daily life. One simplistic idea is that if you do wholesome things you won't go to jail, but if you do unwholesome things you can end up in jail. Based on this distinction, it is not always really clear what is wholesome and what is unwholesome. We know that some people do good things and end up in jail, and some people do evil things and remain free. Someone might steal a thousand dollars and go to prison, and another may steal an election and become the president. Someone commits murder and is executed, while another massacres ten thousand and is a hero. So how useful is to say that unwholesome people go to jail and wholesome people do not?

Because it is not always clear what is wholesome and what is unwholesome, Buddhism prescribes the ten virtues as guides for living. Although three of the virtues pertain to actions, four pertain to speech, and three pertain to the mind, Buddhism gives greatest emphasis to virtues of the mind because the impulses to act or speak arise in the mind. You can usually tell whether someone's actions and speech are wholesome, but it is not as easy to tell if their thoughts are.

In daily life we can usually recognize unwholesome states, but it's another matter when we meditate. Without proper training and practice, it is hard to recognize the unwholesome states that come up—restlessness, drowsiness, self-doubt, laziness, loss of self-control, scattered mind, and erroneous views. Just about every practitioner experiences them, making it very difficult to attain samadhi. On retreat you may experience these problems, but with diligence your mind will gradually stabilize and relax; you will become more settled and more alert; your enthusiasm will overcome laziness, and meditating becomes very rewarding.

There is a difference between laziness and lack of self-control. When you are lazy you may be passively idling and scattered, but when you lack self-control you are actively engaging in incorrect views. You may even lose control over body and mind. But if you make an effort to become stable and relaxed, you will gain control, overcome scattering, and give rise to correct views. The point of practice is to diminish vexations. When your mind is stable, you will perceive its subtler vexations more clearly; recognizing them, you can avoid unwholesome states and give rise to wholesome states. At that point you are actually practicing the Four Proper Exertions.

Most people would assert that they are good, though they are not always clear about what is wholesome and unwholesome. Someone once told me, "Religions teach people to become wholesome. I know that."

I asked him why he had no religion then. He said, "I do not need religion; I never do bad things; I never have bad thoughts. Only people who have bad thoughts and do bad things need religion."

I said, "So you are really a good person, you really have a good heart?"

He said, "Of course I have a good heart."

When I questioned him further, he said, "How dare you question me? What evidence do you have that I am not a good person, that I have unwholesome thoughts?"

I told him, "Well, right now, you are angry. Isn't that unwholesome?"

Despite being a good person, this man could not recognize his own unwholesome thoughts. Some people think anger is not such a bad thing, especially when they can blame others for making them angry. They will say, "You made me angry." They live in suffering and vexation without even knowing it. Some people become angry when they don't get what they want, blaming others or saying that life is unfair. But if they do get what they want, they want more. Some are envious if others are better off, but if they find themselves better off than others, they become proud. Are these wholesome states of mind? You will probably think, "That's just normal!" [*Laughter*]

From the Buddhist perspective, this is vexation and suffering. The purpose of Buddhadharma is to turn suffering into true happiness, vexation into wisdom, anger into compassion, and greed into a loving heart. We use wholesome states to correct what is unwholesome and to cultivate a genuinely pure and stable mind. Without meditation it is difficult to see clearly one's own wholesome and unwholesome states, and to know when the mind is pure or impure. But with meditation practice, your mind becomes stable, clear, and able to see its own subtleties. You will recognize and correct unwholesome states as they arise. For these reasons meditation is a foundation for practicing the Four Proper Exertions. The *Mahaprajnaparamita Shastra* says that practicing the Four Foundations of Mindfulness will eventually give rise to wisdom.

The Five Hindrances

Laxity gives rise to the five hindrances, or obstructions, of desire, anger, sloth, restlessness, and doubt. These five hindrances are in fact unwholesome states that prevent the wholesome faculties of faith, diligence, mindfulness, concentration, and wisdom. These five wholesome faculties are virtuous roots that we plant in our mind, which can then grow into the five corresponding powers of faith, diligence, mindfulness, concentration, and wisdom. (This will be discussed further in chapter 4.)

In life, people desire money, fame, food, love, and living comforts, but what do we desire when we meditate? Surely, they should not be the same things.

Student: Enlightenment, bliss, good feeling.

Sheng Yen: Is this what we are seeking the whole time we are meditating? "When am I going to get enlightened?" "I want supernatural powers." "I want to be at one with the universe." These are desires for extraordinary experiences, or for comfort and bliss while meditating. These attitudes will not get you samadhi, much less wisdom, because they are still desires. Not getting what you want can lead to anger or disgust. The mind will become restless, the body hot and bothered, and the cushion will feel like a volcano. Instead of getting up from the cushion, people like this will keep struggling, looking for something they can't get, or got and lost, and create more and more vexations.

After struggling like this, you have lost energy and you are tired. This obstruction is sloth or torpor, which is characterized by severe drowsiness. So after sleeping on the cushion for a while, like drifting in a rowboat, you recover from tiredness and begin meditating again. But then desire and anger come up again, the mind becomes restless, and the internal struggle begins all over. This is the fourth hindrance, restlessness or being scatter-minded.

A restless mind leads to the fifth hindrance, doubt. Doubt can be lack of confidence in your teacher, or in the method that you learned. Another doubt is to think that because you have problems with your health, your body is not suitable for meditation. With doubts like these, eventually you may decide, "Meditation is not for me."

These five hindrances can obstruct the path to wisdom and compassion. Although they are normal, we can prevent them from becoming serious if we diligently return to the Four Foundations. Better yet, with continuous practice, obstructions will not have a chance to come up in the first place—we will cease unwholesome states and not allow new ones.

The Five Wholesome Faculties

The Four Foundations of Mindfulness help us to give rise to the wholesome faculties of faith, diligence, mindfulness, concentration, and wisdom. Let's consider faith. There are several reasons why we can have faith in something. First, we can have blind faith in something because others also do, or someone tells us to. I once asked someone why he was a Buddhist. He said, "My wife wouldn't marry me unless I became a Buddhist, so I became a Buddhist." This is blind faith, but it is not necessarily bad. This man eventually became a good practitioner.

You can also have faith in something you understand. When you learn the principles of a belief and find them suitable, your belief is based on understanding, not just blind faith. Very often Westerners, especially intellectuals, turn to Buddhism because they understand and feel compatible with its ideas.

Another basis for confidence is firsthand experience. When you put Buddhism into practice and find that it improves your life, stabilizes your mind, and helps you to help others, this builds confidence and faith in Buddhism. This kind of faith is the first wholesome faculty.

The Four Foundations are a path to samadhi, but samadhi by itself does not give rise to wisdom. The Four Foundations emphasize going beyond stilling the mind, and diligently practicing contemplation to arouse the wholesome faculties. Through the second wholesome faculty, diligence, we can eliminate vexation and attain wisdom; without diligence, arousing the wholesome faculties would be very hard. When faith arises, diligence will naturally arise with it. Seeing the results of practice, one will work hard to keep getting good results—this is diligence.

The third wholesome faculty is mindfulness—always keeping the practice foremost in your mind. More than thirty of you took the Three Refuges today, but will it be two years before I see you again? If that happens, you have not given rise to mindfulness, and maybe you will have forgotten the practice. So to be mindful, remind yourself that practicing Dharma is very important and very useful. If you do this ceaselessly, you will become diligent in your practice. And being diligent, you will be able to enter samadhi and eventually give rise to wisdom.

A student did a seven-day retreat with me and then didn't show again for another five years. I asked him, "How come I haven't seen you in five years?" He said, "Shifu, at least I came back. Some people never do."

I have already covered the two remaining wholesome faculties—concentration and wisdom—in depth in the Four Foundations of Mindfulness. Also, both of these faculties are important in the remaining practices of the Thirty-seven Aids, and they will again be covered in depth. But of the five wholesome faculties, diligence is most important to realizing the Four Proper Exertions.

Diligence and the Practice of the Four Proper Exertions

To practice the Four Proper Exertions well, we need virtuous roots. The seeds of virtuous roots are planted when we hear the Dharma. After we hear the Dharma and begin to practice, the Dharma seeds will sprout and give rise to virtuous roots. These new roots can then grow and take shape in our heart-mind. The roots develop and grow branches, and when they are finally above ground, leaves begin to appear. Through the virtuous deeds of practice we can give rise to virtuous roots, but it all begins with seeds being planted when we hear the Dharma. Even as you listen to this Dharma talk, you are collecting seeds that will germinate and grow in your heart-mind. When that happens, it will encourage the growth of your character and raise your spirituality to a higher level.

In the beginning of the path, one has heard the Dharma but has not practiced deeply. This is the ordinary practitioner, which includes most people. At the next stage, one has developed deep virtuous roots, character, and spirituality at a high level, even though there are still vexations. This is the level of a sage. At the third stage, one is a very accomplished practitioner who has eliminated vexations to the point where one no longer harms oneself or others. At the level of a saint or arhat there may arise in the mind subtle vexations, perhaps residual habit tendencies even from previous lives, which no longer manifest as unwholesome thoughts or acts. For such beings, these would be dharmas without outflows. Without diligently practicing the Four Proper Exertions, we cannot expect to get beyond the level of the ordinary practitioner. But when we practice the Dharma and allow virtuous roots to develop in our heart, eventually we can become sages. With continued diligence, we become saints and leave our vexations behind. People may think practice only means sitting meditation, but doing prostrations, reciting the Buddha's name, and reading and reciting sutras are all practices as well.

We can use analogies to describe diligence in practice. There is the diligence of the mother who thinks about her child even when she is away from the child. There is also the diligence of a hen sitting on an egg; she won't say, "Well, I'll just take a few days off, and come back later." Third is the diligence of a baby who wants to keep nursing. These analogies reflect the attitudes we should have: like the mother, we should be mindful of the practice; like the hen, we should persist in the practice; like the baby, we should hunger for practice. Whatever methods you practice, with these attitudes you will have diligence, and you will cultivate virtuous roots.

Diligence is important because it gives us the courage and strength to deal with our own laziness and to succeed in the practice. Practicing the Four Proper Exertions can eliminate laxity, which hinders the development of the wholesome faculties. Diligence will help us complete whatever we do, even as we are confronted with obstacles. That is why we need courage and strength—so that we won't give up easily.

The *Mahaprajnaparamita Shastra* speaks of diligence of the body and diligence of the mind. Diligence of the body refers to using our bodies so that we become more capable of helping others. Diligence of the mind is about cutting off attachments such as greed and desire so we can eliminate laziness. Only when we can begin to control these attachments can we eliminate unwholesomeness. *The Treatise on Consciousness-Only* speaks of diligence in which making and keeping vows is like wearing armor that protects our practice from harm. To develop this armor, one needs courage and strength.

Then there is the diligence that comes through the bodhisattva practice of the Six Paramitas (generosity, morality, patience, diligence, meditation, and wisdom). Bodhisattvas do not say, "I practiced hard for a few days and I'm tired, so I will take a break." No, they will just keep up their practice with no thought of the difficulties. The first four paramitas lead us to the fifth, meditation, which is needed for cultivating samadhi. After that, the sixth paramita of wisdom can arise. Samadhi is not just about sitting still on a cushion; it is about living in the world without being defiled by it. The true samadhi is that which leads us to wisdom. But what is wisdom? Wisdom is about transcending distinctions between right and wrong, between good and bad, while still dealing with things appropriately. It is being able to deal with subjects and objects while transcending subject/object distinctions.

For practitioners, not only can the body become tired but more subtly, the mind can become weary of the practice. Diligence is needed to keep that from happening. Some people think they can just jump into the practice, and samadhi will come and wisdom will arise. After practicing for a while without experiencing samadhi and wisdom, there is a good chance they will lose faith and give up. This is because they lack diligence. Some practice for a year or two, or even ten years or more, and then give up. That is already pretty good, because they actually practiced for a while. Or some will say that they'll practice harder the next time around, in the next life. Even that is not too bad, if they sincerely believe they will practice in their next life. All these people can help themselves by practicing the Four Proper Exertions.

The diligence of helping other sentient beings arises out of compassion that does not let up. There are people such as social workers who burn out after working very hard to help people. However, a bodhisattva takes the view that helping others takes place over many lifetimes, but in the process one also helps oneself. It is not how much talent we have, but how diligent we are. Even if you are not now engaged in spreading Dharma, if you can make a vow to help in the future, you will at least have the idea of offering yourself. This of course is the third of the Four Proper Exertions: to give rise to wholesome activity not yet arisen. But without diligence, your vow will not last long.

In one of the sutras, there is this statement: "Being slothful, one falls into unwholesomeness; to avoid sloth, practice diligence." When we are lazy, we will fall from practicing wholesome factors into practicing unwholesome factors. For instance, we may easily fall from practicing samadhi into becoming emotionally afflicted, confused, or depressed. People tend to do things in the opposite direction of diligence. If we can get rid of this habit, we can all become great bodhisattvas. But because we all have these habits, we remain ordinary sentient beings.

We must not misunderstand: being diligent does not mean being overly zealous; it means persisting, ceaselessly working hard in our practice. There are two meanings here. The first applies to sitting meditation: when we sit, we should continuously bring our mind back to the method, continuously staying on the method. The second meaning applies to daily life. For example, tonight if you have a chore that you haven't finished and you're sleepy, does that mean you forgo sleep? No, if you're tired, you sleep. If you are hungry, get something to eat. If you're thirsty, get something to drink. But after you have rested, after you have eaten, after you have something to drink, go back and finish your chore. This is the attitude of ceaselessly trying to get the job done, not taking a break whenever you feel like it. This attitude toward practice is a lifetime commitment. It is not something that you can try for a while and then quit, or just move on to other interests. This would not be diligence.

Diligence Is a Daily Habit

Constant diligence is not only for monks and nuns but laypeople as well. Remind yourself every day what you should do and then do it. Develop the daily habit of doing what you should do and not doing what you should not do. When you are doing what you shouldn't, tell yourself to stop it; when you are doing what you should, tell yourself to continue. If your mind is vexed, give yourself time and effort to quiet it. To quiet your mind, make it a habit to put aside some time every morning to meditate, prostrate, or recite a sutra. All day, from moment to moment, tell yourself not to allow unwholesome thoughts to arise, and if they do, vow not to give rise to them again. If unwholesome thoughts get stronger, meditate. If you don't deal with them early, they may get stronger and manifest as unwholesome actions.

When strong negative thoughts come up, you can practice repentance or prostration, or both. Practicing repentance means reflecting on your past and current behavior, and giving rise to genuine feelings of regret and remorse for any unwholesome patterns. If you have broken any precepts, this is a good time to reaffirm them. Your repentance practice may also include doing prostrations in order not only to express humility, but to practice loosening the hold of ego on your thoughts and behavior. During retreats, when we practice repentance, we will finish by doing twenty minutes of prostrations before the altar. At home you may prostrate to an image of a buddha or bodhisattva in order to focus your mind.

But it is not necessary to prostrate before any image of any kind. The main thing is to see prostration as another method of meditation that can help lead to liberation. Just keep your mind clear and focused only on the act of prostrating.

As you use these methods over time, unwholesome mental habits will arise less and less. Do not expect to experience absolutely no unwholesome states any time soon. If your mind were totally pure, you would already be an arhat. But with diligence you will continue to reduce the occurrence of unwholesome states.

Diligence and Desire

The *Sutra of Forty-two Chapters* says that followers who are not deluded by desire, who are not bothered by countless devious things, and who vigorously cultivate the unconditioned, will attain the Way. "Diligence"—vigorous cultivation—here means precisely that one should not allow oneself to be confused by feelings of desire, or misled by devious ideas. If you can do this ceaselessly, you will attain liberation from suffering and vexation.

What desires are we talking about? For home-leavers they include any kind of sexual desire; for laypeople they refer to sexual misconduct outside of marriage. For example, if you already have a partner, desiring another will result in suffering for oneself and others. Humans are driven by more than biological needs; they are also driven by psychological needs for more sex and more partners. I know a married man who has so many girlfriends you can't count them. He fights with his wife all the time and says he is ready for a divorce. He says, "Who cares if I get divorced, I still have all these girlfriends." I asked him, "If you get a divorce and marry one of your girlfriends, wouldn't you fight with her as well?" He said, "It doesn't matter. I'll get divorced again."

People like this are ruled by desire. At first glance, they seem to get a lot of happiness from having many partners. However, they also suffer. Think about it: do they actually have more happiness or more suffering?

The myriad devious things that the sutra talks about refer not only to acts, but thoughts as well. For example, it is devious to expect to get a lot of money without working hard for it, to believe that all it takes is some smart ideas. Although this is sometimes possible, if making money means using dishonest means that hurt people, this is not only devious but also immoral.

There was a group of youngsters in Taiwan who would break into homes and steal everything. When they got caught, a Buddhist monk went to the jail to teach them some Dharma. This master told them, "Why don't you get jobs instead of robbing people?" Their reply was, "We have jobs. Our job is stealing. It's hard work. We have to do a lot of research and planning before we rob a house. This time we were unlucky and got caught. Next time we'll do a better job." I won't tell you the rest of the story, but I wanted to illustrate a kind of devious thinking—that some people think everybody else is dishonest, and that harming others is right and reasonable.

When I was young and others learned that I was vegetarian, many people tried to induce me to eat meat. Some argued that animals are meant for us to eat, and if we didn't eat them they would multiply, and eventually there wouldn't be any space for us humans. This is another example of devious thinking. My answer was, "That doesn't make any sense. If we didn't raise pigs for food, there wouldn't be so many of them."

Practice like a Stream

Before entering nirvana the Buddha told his followers, "Be diligent in your practice. If you are diligent, there is nothing you cannot accomplish." Think of your practice as a stream. As time goes by, the flowing water will wear down the rocks in its path. Even drops of water falling on a rock will make a hole in the rock if they persist long enough. To use another analogy, being lazy in practice is like rubbing two sticks to start a fire, but quitting before the sticks are even warm. You may have the intention and know-how to start a fire, but if you are not diligent, you won't get the sticks hot enough to ignite.

So diligent practice is like wearing down rocks with water, or making a fire by rubbing sticks. It means ceaselessly taking care of your mind, your speech, and your actions for a very long time. Otherwise you will be just like the camper who wants to start a fire but is too lazy to persevere. Some hear that Buddhism can give them a lot of benefits, so they come and practice sitting meditation a few times and then stop if they don't see quick results. All they get is pain in their legs, they're not allowed to talk, they can't do this and can't do that, and they feel like they're in jail. They don't see any immediate benefits, so they just quit. They want to enjoy the benefits of the practice, but they are impatient and don't want to put in the time. How can they get the fire started if the wood isn't even warm?

The key is diligence. Be like the mother who is always mindful of her child, the hen who patiently sits on her eggs, and the hungry child who always wants to nurse. Being diligent does not mean killing yourself with practicing. It should be gentle, like a stream flowing ceaselessly over rocks for a very long time. It should not be like a torrent of water pouring for a very short time, and then stopping. That can be very harmful to you, possibly to others around you, and you will not realize the benefits of the practice. It is much better to practice like a small stream, continuously flowing for a long time. It should be like this when you practice the Way. That will give you the greatest benefits of the practice.

The Four Proper Exertions in Daily Life

Practicing the Four Proper Exertions can be summarized by two questions you can ask yourself: First, "Am I engaging in unwholesome acts, words, and thoughts?" Second, "Am I engaging in wholesome acts, words, and thoughts?" Basically the Four Proper Exertions are pretty simple. They are attitudes we should have in daily life as well as in practicing the Dharma; they tell us not to do what we should not, and to do what we should. Although most people will agree with this statement, the usual tendency is to recognize the good that we do but not the bad. We think that because we are good people we only do good things. However, we are all born with negative energies that propel our actions, following us from birth to death. Some of us are less aware of these habitual tendencies than others.

I know this woman who talks very loudly. When talking in a group she is even louder. One day I told her that she talked too loudly while in the temple. She said, "I can't help it. I was born with this voice." She didn't see her habit as a problem, even when it bothered others. Some people know they are being difficult; others are not only unaware, but when they are told that they are being difficult, they think it's not their problem.

In Taiwan, our Dharma Drum Mountain organization had a help-wanted ad in the paper and this man applied. His resume showed that on average, he changed jobs about every two months. We asked him why he changed jobs so frequently. He said, "This is a dog-eat-dog world. Wherever I work, people are mean to me, so I always have to leave." I said, "Why would you want to work here if you might leave before you even learn the job?" He said, "Oh, this is different. It is a mean world out there, but here you people are compassionate." I told him, "We are just ordinary people. You will have to understand what's causing you to change jobs so frequently. It's up to you to do something about it." So we gave him a probation period to see if he could adapt to our environment. The people in the organization were not mean to him nor did they reject him, but after two months he left. He just couldn't adapt. Before he left I told him, "You know, it is not true that everybody is mean to you. It is really a negative attitude that makes you see everybody as taking advantage of you. As long as you have this attitude, you will see the world that way." After our talk, he said, "Thanks. Maybe I will find a better place somewhere else." I feel very sorry for people like this, who suffer a great deal all the time.

Those who are more aware try to correct their negative tendencies, but may find that the bad habits persist. They can practice the Four Proper Exertions, which have been emphasized in important sutras ranging from the most ancient to the later Mahayana sutras. In the *Sutra of Forty-two Chapters*, it is said that "Constantly observing the 250 precepts, practitioners enter and abide in purity. By practicing the four true paths, they will attain the stage of arhats." Spoken to home-leavers, that is to say, people who have taken monastic vows, this sutra says that only by diligently observing the precepts, always abiding in purity, and practicing the Four Noble Truths, will they attain liberation as arhats. In other words, for monastics following the Mahayana path, all of these together constitute practicing the Four Proper Exertions. While lay practitioners are not required to take all the precepts of monastics, they still need to uphold the five basic precepts, and they should still practice the Four Proper Exertions with diligence.

Some rare practitioners can become arhats in one lifetime after hearing the Dharma; most take much longer. Even to accomplish it in several lifetimes requires great diligence. Without diligence, it will probably never happen. Not being diligent means practicing sometimes, sometimes not, one day feeling, "I will practice today," and another day, "I think I'll skip it." Real diligence means practicing continuously without ceasing.

3

THE FOUR STEPS
TO MAGICAL POWERS

THE FOUR STEPS to Magical Powers are also called by names such as the Four Steps to the Power of Ubiquity, the Four Steps to Unlimited Power, and the Four Kinds of Samadhi. The Sanskrit term *riddhipada* means "steps to power." Its Chinese term, *si ru yi zu*, speaks of a mind that can accomplish whatever it wants to. This is a mind that is master of itself, free and at ease.

There is a Chinese saying, "Eight out of nine things that happen to us do not match our expectations." Why does so much of what happens to us not match our expectations? It is because we are usually not the master of our own mind. We think about what we should not, and we can't bring ourselves to think about what we should. Both habits contribute to our not gaining control of our lives. We do not learn from the past and have no clear plan for the future, and therefore we continue to make mistakes. Constantly faced with problems, our life is filled with adversity. Not being able to control our mind, we let small problems become big problems; not being able to reach our goals, we are ill at ease. However, with correct practice we can gradually eliminate these obstacles, and then more will happen according to our expectations.

The Four Enhanced Phenomena

The Mahayana path to buddhahood can be likened to a journey of five stages. In the first stage we gather the provisions we will need for the journey. In terms of the path, this means practicing the Four Foundations of Mindfulness and the Four Proper Exertions. In the second stage we actually set off on the path to buddhahood. This stage consists in practicing the Four Steps to Magical Powers, and it is characterized by the four enhanced phenomena. The third stage is realizing dhyana, in which one directly perceives that the true nature of the self is that of a buddha. This is the stage of the arhat, or saint. The fourth stage is to actualize the bodhisattva path in which one practices dhyana to realize samadhi and wisdom. This enables one to use skillful means to deliver sentient beings. The fifth stage of the journey is complete liberation in buddhahood.

Before talking about the Four Steps to Magical Powers, I want to briefly describe what are called the four enhanced phenomena. In the progressive view of practice, one begins with the Four Foundations of Mindfulness and proceeds to the Four Proper Exertions. At the point of being able to practice both together, one is close to being able to experience the four enhanced phenomena: warmth, summit, forbearance, and supreme in the world. These phenomena grow out of one's practice and validate that one has indeed planted virtuous roots. "Warmth" means that one's mind is becoming soft and gentle, and that harshness is receding. "Summit" means that having gotten rid of harshness, one's mind has ascended to the peak, so to speak. "Forbearance" means one will not cause harm to oneself or others. "Supreme in the world" means one has transcended worldliness and is approaching the stage of an arhat. These phenomena are skillful means that one applies to one's practice, and they are cumulative. For example, the stage of summit also includes the stage of warmth, and so on. At the stage of supreme in the world, one has attained the skillful means that may take them all the way to enlightenment. For the purpose of the Four Steps to Power, summit is the most appropriate to discuss.

At the level of summit, one's mind has become soft and gentle, not just sometimes but at all times. People often mistakenly assume that if one can enter samadhi, one's problems will go away. Another misunderstanding is to expect that having had a glimpse of enlightenment, one will no longer have vexations. The truth is that only when wisdom and dhyana arise together are we at a stage where we will not cause vexation to ourselves or others. Until then, though we may be at ease with a joyous mind, we are not yet liberated because we are still attached to the idea of a self. To attain the summit level is not really that high, but it is still very good. It speaks of spiritual power, and it is at this level that we begin the practice of the riddhipada.

Two Kinds of Power

It is possible to generate two kinds of power through the riddhipada. The first is supernatural powers, through which one can transcend ordinary physical limitations. Examples would be the ability to transport oneself to different places and times, to perform alchemy, or to become invisible. If you were invisible you could take whatever you wanted and not get caught. Would this be stealing? I guess you could call it magical stealing. [*Laughter*] One could become rich without working. But if you had such supernatural powers, would you use them that way? I think not. These are not the kinds of powers one would use on the dhyana path.

The second kind of power one can generate is freedom and ease of mind. To attain that state we practice dhyana, which is the reason the Four Steps to Magical Power are also called the Four Kinds of Samadhi. There are differences between the non-Buddhist and the Buddhist practices of samadhi. In non-Buddhist meditation, one's goal is to stop wandering thoughts, to enter samadhi, and to experience freedom from vexation. However, coming out of samadhi, one will again experience wandering thoughts and vexation. So life is good in samadhi, not so good out of it.

The Buddhist approach is different because we first practice the Four Foundations of Mindfulness and the Four Proper Exertions. Through these contemplations we generate wisdom. Whether or not we enter samadhi, we can still use this wisdom to lessen our vexations and to reduce conflicts and contradictions within our mind. This is why we begin with the Four Foundations and Four Proper Exertions. Buddhism emphasizes the need to practice in order to realize one's own buddha-nature. This does not mean that someone who perceives buddha-nature is no longer subject to vexation. After experiencing buddha-nature for the first time, one still has habits and propensities that can lead to impure thoughts and impure conduct; greed and aversion may still arise. However, one is at least able to see clearly that one's mind still cannot completely control the arising of vexations. At that point it becomes very important to practice samadhi.

To summarize, in the stages of practice toward enlightenment, we cultivate wisdom through contemplation, and when wisdom arises, we practice samadhi to develop freedom and ease. This is the kind of power we want to develop through the Four Steps to Magical Powers, not supernatural powers.

The Four Steps to Magical Powers are (1) *chanda*, concentration of desire; (2) *virya*, concentration of exertion; (3) *chitta*, concentration of mind; and (4) *mimamsa*, concentration of inquiry, or investigation.

Chanda, concentration of desire, is the will to attain the wondrous and supreme dhyana where wisdom manifests. This intense longing will cause one to prepare one's mind accordingly and inspire one to practice hard. When *chanda* is translated into Chinese, the term can have a negative as well as a positive meaning.

On the one hand it can mean greed, but as a step to concentrative power, chanda also denotes a hope or vow to attain the supreme dhyana. This vow is essential in order to overcome the six obstructions to practice: drowsiness, scattered mind, idleness, laziness, forgetfulness, and wrong view. The will to attain the supreme dhyana is the best antidote to laziness. So when you are practicing and begin to feel lazy, please give rise to the aspiration to attain the supreme dhyana.

Virya, concentration of exertion, means one is equipped with a strong vow to attain the supreme dhyana, and therefore one diligently applies the method of practice. We have discussed the Four Proper Exertions as correct attitudes while practicing the Four Foundations of Mindfulness to give rise to wisdom, and here we use the attitude of the Four Proper Exertions to give rise to diligence in dhyana.

Chitta, concentration of mind, means to be focused on the practice of dhyana. We have spoken of the need to practice dhyana diligently. But what do we use to practice dhyana? We use the mind of the present moment, keeping the mind on the present moment and only on the present moment. This is the mind that gives rise to dhyana, or wisdom. The mind of ordinary sentient beings is selfish and full of vexation. Even so, it is this same mind that we practice with, and it is the same mind as that of an arhat. However, when we start practicing dhyana, we cannot become pure immediately; we still have wandering thoughts, impure thoughts, and selfish thoughts. Originally the mind is scattered, but when it is continuously on the method, it is on the path to dhyana.

Mimamsa, concentration of inquiry, means using wisdom to observe whether our mind is in the proper state. As we said, the proper state is summit, where the entire mind is soft and gentle, without harshness. If we see that the mind is selfish and impure, then it is not in the proper state and we need to correct it right away. In practicing dhyana, we encounter the five hindrances or obstructions. As long as there is one obstruction remaining, it is not the proper state of mind and not the right way to practice dhyana. Therefore, when we speak of the proper state of mind for meditation, we also mean the absence of self-centered thoughts.

At the stage of practicing the Four Steps to Magical Powers, one focuses on eliminating laziness. We talked earlier about the strong will to practice the supreme dhyana as a way to overcome laziness. Here we also speak of observing whether one has the proper state of mind as a way of dealing with laziness.

We have talked about supreme in the world, where one is liberated from samsara as an arhat. Though the mind will no longer give rise to unwholesome activity or vexation, there still remain residual habit-energies until one attains buddhahood. In other words, there are still subtle obstructions. When all obstructions have finally been overcome, one has attained buddhahood.

Practicing the Four Steps to Magical Powers

So far we talked about the Four Steps as mainly the practice of samadhi. Now I am going to talk about how we go about this practice. Only those who have cultivated deep samadhi and who have attained the four dhyanas and eight samadhis have magical powers that they can control. One who has mastered real supernatural power can perform otherworldly feats at will. Even so, having these powers does not mean one is liberated in the Buddhist sense. It may sound appealing, but in fact these powers are not always useful and often yield negative results; they are not in themselves reliable and are often illusory. For instance, people may use supernatural powers to visit the past or foresee the future, or to witness things happening elsewhere. They may see concealed objects or read other people's minds. Abilities like these may seem useful, but they mainly serve to give pleasure and pride to the user. From the perspective of the present, seeing into the future may seem useful. However, the future is really determined by causes and conditions and by causes and consequences; what will or will not happen is determined by karma. Trying to change one's karma with supernatural powers would not work, since that would violate the law of karma.

In both the early Buddhist and Mahayana traditions, there are records of supernatural powers being used. But what did the Buddha do when he was hungry? Did he conjure up a feast, or have one catered by a deity? No, he walked around with his alms bowl begging for food. After he attained buddhahood he walked from village to village spreading the Dharma. He did not fly through the air. He did not magically erect monasteries, but relied on laypeople to build them and to sew robes for the sangha. Before entering parinirvana—you may have read of this—he received an offering of food that was tainted. You would think that he should have used his supernatural powers to know the food was bad, but he did eat it and became very sick. So even though the Buddha possessed supernatural powers, he did not use them in self-centered ways.

One of the Buddha's senior disciples, Maudgalyayana, was noted for his magic and clairvoyance. Among the Buddha's disciples was one called Color of Lotus, who was famous for her supernatural powers. Both of these disciples were ultimately beaten to death by people hostile to Buddhism. You could say that because they had supernatural powers, they should have escaped from their attackers. But they couldn't, because having supernatural powers does not change one's karma.

I want to emphasize again that we practice dhyana not to acquire supernatural powers, but to attain liberation. We begin the Thirty-seven Aids to Enlightenment with the Four Foundations of Mindfulness to calm our mind, and to become clearly aware of how thoughts rise and fall in our mind. We then practice the Four Proper Exertions along with the Four Foundations, with an attitude of great diligence. Practicing these contemplations together results in the generation of wisdom. However, without adequate samadhi, this wisdom will not be deep-rooted and firm. At this stage we need to develop samadhi power in order for this wisdom to have a secure foundation. To do that, we cultivate dhyana.

I previously described the four enhanced phenomena of warmth, summit, forbearance, and supreme in the world. These phenomena characterize the practice of the Four Steps. I also described the Four Steps to Magical Powers as the second of the five stages to buddhahood. So on the foundation of dhyana, we build our practice, and from this we move forward on the path of the bodhisattvas and buddhas.

One of the main methods of dhyana in Chan is investigating *huatou*. By investigating a huatou, one may make a breakthrough and perceive directly that the nature of self is emptiness and that there is no enduring self. This self-nature is also called buddha-nature. Seeing one's buddha-nature, however, does not mean that one is liberated, nor does it mean that one's practice is completed. Rather, it means that one has gained more faith and confidence in the practice, and that one now clearly knows where the path is. This may be likened to traveling on a dark road on a very dark night. All of a sudden, there is a bolt of lightning. For a split second, you see the road before you, bright and clear. But seeing the road is not the same as having finished the journey. You still need to travel on to the end. In a similar manner, seeing your self-nature may have gained you a little bit of wisdom, but you still need to practice. The next step is to deepen your samadhi, to cultivate dhyana. So actually, the term Four Steps to Magical Power is really an analogy of the stages of meditative concentration. In that sense, a more proper term would be the Four Kinds of Samadhi.

As we have said, chanda is the intense desire to attain dhyana. To develop the power of chanda, one looks at the mind's vexations and contemplates their true nature. Do these vexations have enduring existence? If you contemplate them deeply, you will see that all vexatious thoughts are indeed illusory. Since they are illusory, why attach to them? One will then realize that we suffer because of our attachments to vexations. So the more we observe the mind and the more we realize that our vexations are illusory, the more we can let vexations go. In this practice, we remind ourselves, "I know that wandering thoughts arise because of my attachments, and I know that they cause me vexation." As long as there is attachment, all your thoughts are wandering thoughts. So when you see that wandering thoughts are caused by vexation and cause more vexation, and that one should therefore not attach to them, then you will learn to let them go. When you can do that, they will gradually subside, and your mind will become clearer and more stable, thus enabling dhyana.

Virya is diligence in dealing with the wandering thoughts that arise, whether they are thoughts of the past, present, or future. As for the present, thoughts come and go ceaselessly, and when we attach to them they become wandering thoughts. However, thoughts of the past and future are also wandering thoughts, since the past is gone and the future is yet to be. All wandering thoughts, whether they relate to the past, the present, or the future, are illusory, so we just let them go. When we are diligent in letting go of thoughts of the past, not giving rise to thoughts of the future, and stopping thoughts in the present, we eventually enter the single-minded state of nonabiding. This corresponds to the line in the *Diamond Sutra* that says, "Abiding nowhere, give rise to [awakened] mind."

Chitta is being mindful of your intent to practice. You need to be on guard against laziness, drowsiness, and scattered mind. You need to be aware that these states cause vexation and that they are the reasons we cannot attain liberation. Constantly be aware of their presence, and once aware of them, put them aside right away. Do not struggle with them, as that will make them worse. If you can do this, constantly observing your mind and putting down obstructions, you will be able to attain samadhi, the state of one-thought.

Mimamsa consists of having an inquiring or discerning mind,

ensuring that chanda, virya, and chitta are present. If desire, diligence, and intent are present along with inquiry, it is possible with consistent practice to enter deep samadhi. Mimamsa consists in knowing fully the importance of the other *riddhis* and knowing that the Four Steps to Magical Powers is an important stage on the path to buddhahood.

Practicing any one of the riddhis is a great benefit, but the greatest benefit would be to practice all four. Once you have established a firm footing in one of the riddhis, it is easier to move on to the next. When you have mastered the Four Steps to Magical Powers, the next stage is to fully embark on the path of the bodhisattvas and buddhas. We talked a lot about supernatural powers, but mainly in order to make it clear that the attainment of such powers is not the purpose of dhyana. The true magical power of dhyana is in attaining the path of the bodhisattvas and buddhas. That is what is really useful.

4

THE FIVE ROOTS
AND THE FIVE POWERS

THE FIVE ROOTS are mental faculties that grow out of the cultivation of samadhi through the Four Foundations of Mindfulness,
the Four Proper Exertions, and the Four Steps to Magical Powers.
Thus the Five Roots and the Five Powers make up the fourth and
fifth groups in the Thirty-seven Aids to Enlightenment. Though
they are separate in order of realization, I will discuss them together
because they are integrally related. In other words, there is a causal
relationship because, based on one's practice of the Five Roots, one
can derive the Five Powers.

The Five Roots can be thought of as virtuous roots resulting
from the cultivation of samadhi. These virtues are (1) faith, (2)
diligence, (3) mindfulness, (4) concentration, and (5) wisdom.
They are called virtuous because they are also foundations of
the bodhisattva path. Practicing the five virtuous roots, one can
realize their corresponding powers. For example, cultivating the
roots of faith enhances the power of faith, cultivating the roots
of perseverance enhances the power of perseverance, cultivating
the roots of mindfulness enhances the power of mindfulness,
and so on.

Enhancing the Roots of Faith

To cultivate faith means to enhance the roots of faith, or belief. Difficult as it may be to establish faith, it is equally or more difficult to enhance it. Just telling yourself that you have faith may not be enough to prevent you from regressing. To enhance faith, you need to cultivate it—as you establish the roots of faith, you must also constantly promote their growth. To establish faith, you need to believe in three things: the law of cause and effect, or karma; the law of causes and conditions; and the Three Jewels—the Buddha, the Dharma, and the Sangha.

What does it mean to believe in karma? Karma says that whatever actions we perform will have effects resulting from those actions. Whatever fortune and misfortune and whatever happiness and unhappiness we experience, they are all effects from actions planted in the past. At times we experience effects that are due to causes that we know about, and at other times the causes are too deeply imbedded in the past. Therefore to better understand karma, we must look at it in terms of the past, present, and future. Only when we can think about karma in terms of the three time periods can we arrive at a clear understanding of the law of cause and effect.

Because I believe in karma, I feel that if my time to die has come, it will come no matter where I am or what I am doing. I may die taking a shower or falling downstairs. But if according to karma it is not my time to die, then wherever I go, it will still not be my time to die. If according to karma one's time has really arrived, then one may be in a particular time and place and be affected. The thing to remember is that if we really believe in the law of cause and effect, we do not complain or blame others when we meet adversity. We accept what happens as the result of our karma.

Next, we need to believe in the law of causes and conditions.

This law says that whatever we experience, whether it is security or fear, happiness or sadness, contentment or discontent, results from many causes and conditions coming together. This is also called conditioned arising. It is not a simple and linear process from causes and conditions to effects. Rather, from the initiation of the causes all the way to the fruition of effects, many different conditions come into play, and in the process conditions also change. Even if causes and effects are destined to place one in danger, preventive measures can decrease or even avoid the suffering that would have otherwise occurred. The point is that cultivating virtuous and wholesome deeds can change the process of causes and conditions coming to fruition. Hence it is possible to change one's fate.

In the late nineties, there were heavy floods in Taiwan. In a certain area two towns were hit by the floods. In one town, so many people died that many of the bodies could not be found. In the other town, many houses and buildings were destroyed, but no one died at all. In the first town they had no prior experience of this kind of disaster, so they were not alert to the potential danger, and as a result they suffered greatly. In the second town they had prior experience, so when they received the flood alert, they quickly evacuated, thus saving lives. In this story we can see how causes and conditions made a difference in the two situations.

If you have truly established and maintained a solid faith in karma and conditioned arising, there is no reason to be afraid and to feel insecure. If you truly believe in these two laws and it is really your time to die, there is no use panicking. And if it is not your time to die, why be fearful? On the other hand, if you believe in conditioned arising, you would try to minimize the dangerous elements in your life. You would not foolishly put yourself in harm's way and you would take measures to avoid danger.

During the earthquake in Taiwan in September 1999, many Buddhist monasteries were damaged. However, not one person died in these monasteries. I asked some of the survivors how they escaped danger, and their response was that when the temples collapsed, they did not panic. They kept calm and were able to find a way out of the rubble. When some of the other buildings collapsed, people may have panicked and thus lost their lives.

However, you can take all the preventive measures you want, but if it's your time, you may die even if there is no apparent danger present. With this kind of understanding, you will not feel so much fear in uncertain circumstances. You will feel more secure, live more safely, and perhaps a little longer. If you are constantly fearful, anxious, and insecure about what is going on, you might even put your life in jeopardy as a result.

When we believe in conditioned arising, we are not disappointed by setbacks nor are we arrogant in success. We understand that as causes and conditions change, favorable conditions can easily turn unfavorable, and vice versa. When we believe firmly in the law of causes and conditions, we can face reality and use wisdom to deal with changing events.

In addition to believing in karma and conditioned arising, we need to believe in the Three Jewels, which are the Buddha, the Dharma, and the Sangha. The Buddha is the enlightened being who has shown us the way out of suffering. We need to have faith in the Buddha because he is one who traveled the path before us and whose footsteps we wish to follow.

The Dharma is the actual teachings of the Buddha that we also call Buddhadharma. The Four Noble Truths, the law of karma, the law of causes and conditions, as well as the Thirty-seven Aids to Enlightenment, are all examples of Buddhadharma. As long as we know the Dharma and apply it properly, we can handle problems we encounter. In this sense, the most important of the jewels is the Dharma. Using it to regulate our thoughts, we can achieve peace of mind; using it to regulate our behavior, we can find security in daily life. Practicing Dharma helps us modify our behavior in positive ways, thus establishing better causes and conditions for ourselves and others. If one can truly follow the Dharma, there's really nothing one should be fearful about.

Finally, if we want to learn and use the Dharma properly, we need the third jewel, the Sangha, or monastic community, which helps to insure proper transmission of the teachings. It also provides a disciplined practice environment and the means for the members to encourage each other.

If they sound useful to you, please apply these ideas about enhancing the roots of faith to your daily life; learn to be more careful rather than more fearful. Rather than panicking in the face of potential danger, take wise preventive measures.

Student: I can understand using the concept of karma and past, present, and future lives to avoid worry and fear. The problem is, my co-workers do not believe in Buddhist principles. How should I approach helping these people?

Sheng Yen: Use your wisdom to encourage people to use their own wisdom. I teach people to handle problems in everyday life with four simple rules. When you encounter a problem, first, face it; second, accept it; third, deal with it; and fourth, put it down. Facing it means that whatever happened has already happened and there's no use denying it, so one ought to just face it. And since you are willing to face it, you should accept the reality of what has happened. Once you accept it, you can use wisdom to deal with the situation. And after dealing with the situation, you should no longer worry about it or be fearful; you should put it down, let it go.

These four principles are very useful, and you could apply them to helping people. You can encourage others to use this method without the need to talk about Buddhism. After the 1999 earthquake I referred to the victims as bodhisattvas. By that I meant that their sacrifice helped the rest of us by teaching us how to take better preventive measures, thus improving our safety and our lives. We can see victims of disasters as bodhisattvas helping us to alleviate suffering, especially those who gave their lives to help others. This perspective in understanding their deaths is both more compassionate and more respectful.

As we have said, the Five Roots are called virtues because they lay a strong foundation for our future practice. Each root has its own function, which can be expressed as one of the corresponding powers. For example, the virtuous root of faith gives rise to the power of faith, and so on. One can readily understand that a plant with roots that are deep, big, and strong will have a better chance for survival and growth than one with small, fragile roots. Similarly, if our virtuous roots are not deep and strong, we can easily be influenced by our environment and forget or even lose our vow to practice. Therefore, to cultivate wisdom and compassion we need to strengthen these five virtuous roots, also called roots without outflows. The Dharma without outflows is the Dharma of liberation; hence it is through cultivating the Five Roots that one moves toward liberation.

How do we cultivate these Five Roots without outflows? We begin by practicing the Four Foundations of Mindfulness, and then we apply the wholesome diligence of the Four Proper Exertions. Next, we use the virtue derived from the Four Proper Exertions to cultivate the Four Steps to Magical Powers. After firmly establishing these practices, one has gained the wisdom of contemplation as well as samadhi. At that point one's faith will be very strong. So in fact we lay the foundation of the Five Roots when we begin to practice the Four Foundations of Mindfulness. Therefore it is important to understand that the Five Roots and the Five Powers are intimately related to the earlier stages of the Thirty-seven Aids. It is not as if the Five Roots just emerged out of nowhere.

A young man asked me, "Shifu, how can I not be influenced by the temptations in the environment?"

I told him, "You must see the environment as having nothing to do with you. That way you will not be tempted by what goes on."

And he said, "I understand."

So he sounds like he understands, but mere understanding is not enough because when things occur in the environment, we will still be tempted, and our mind will still be swayed by that.

Two days ago someone came to me and wanted to discuss Buddhadharma. I told him that one can learn about Buddhism through books and teachers, but knowing all those concepts and theories is not by itself useful. It is not enough for improving one's daily life and one's character. It is like going to a restaurant very hungry and just studying the menu without ordering anything. Unless you actually eat one of the dishes, you will still be hungry. Or if you work at a bank, handling a lot of other people's money does not make you rich. Studying, reading, and talking about Buddhist ideas are not helpful at all if you only experience them intellectually.

My own teacher, Master Dongchu, said that manifesting one line of teaching in your conduct is better than speaking ten lines of Dharma. What we're talking about is actually practicing the Dharma. So without practice, one's roots will not be deep; they will remain very shallow, never firm. Therefore, without practice it will be very difficult to not be affected by temptations in the environment.

Since coming to America in 1975, I have given numerous talks on sutras, shastras, and all sorts of Buddhist topics, and I have held many retreats. As a result, many people have listened to the Dharma that I have spoken. However, relatively few of them seriously practice the Dharma, and of those people not very many can stay with it and persevere. Yet among those who practiced with me at the beginning, many are still with me. Actually some of them are here today, so it's pretty remarkable. Thank you. So in twenty-plus years I actually did something. These people are still here because they have enhanced their faith through participation in many intensive retreats. They have gained experiences that have stabilized and calmed their minds and helped them in daily life.

Many students also disappear for periods of time but come back, showing that their faith has strong and deep roots. Again, the reason is mostly because they have understood the benefits of practice and because they have been applying Buddhadharma to their life. No matter how much one knows of Buddhist concepts, unless one uses them in daily life one is not really practicing. Under these conditions it is very difficult to strengthen one's faith.

Enhancing the Roots of Diligence

The second of the Five Roots and Five Powers is diligence, or perseverance. We have already discussed diligence in the context of the Four Proper Exertions, but here we want to talk about how understanding wholesomeness and unwholesomeness can enhance our diligence. Earlier we discussed wholesomeness as being the ten virtues, and unwholesomeness as being their opposite, the ten nonvirtues. We usually talk about wholesome and unwholesome in relative terms—we say that something is wholesome or unwholesome compared to something else. For example, most people who have never been in jail may think they are more wholesome than someone who has. But what does wholesome mean in absolute terms? Absolute wholesomeness refers to a mind that is not moved by the environment at all, and that requires one's cultivation of wisdom and samadhi be complete. And what is unwholesome in absolute terms? We can think of deeds such as killing, arson, rape; these deeds we see as unwholesome in the extreme, and in that sense, they are absolute. My point is, from the point of view of practice, it is not enough to just focus on being relatively wholesome. We should also strive to attain absolute wholesomeness.

Once I was sitting under a tree in a park when a young man approached me. He stood behind me and said, "Don't move."

I thought he was going to mug me or something. Next he clapped his hands very loudly right behind my head.

I turned around and asked him, "What are you doing?"

He said, "There was this huge mosquito by your head, so I killed it."

I told him that maybe he was doing a good deed for me, but the mosquito just wanted a little bit of blood, and he took its life.

He said to me, "In this world, everything that isn't good is bad for human beings."

I told him, "From the mosquito's point of view, human beings are just one food source. There's nothing good or bad about it."

In terms of common sense, this young man had good intentions, and you could say his action was relatively wholesome. However, his discriminatory mind saw human life as more precious than that of insects, and from this perspective his behavior was unwholesome in the absolute sense.

This young man may be an example of the mind following the environment. Usually our mind is moved and turned by what's going on around us. When that happens the mind is in an unwholesome state. On the other hand, when the mind is very clear and calm and not affected by the environment, that is a wholesome mind. Furthermore, the environment itself can be changed by a wholesome mind. In daily life, as events move our mind, we should recognize right away that our mind is in an unwholesome state and then act accordingly. That is to say, we should avoid actions, thoughts, and words that would further stimulate the unwholesome state. We should strive to move toward a wholesome mind, thus allowing the environment to follow the mind.

Unwholesomeness occurs when we give rise to vexations that cause suffering to ourselves and others. To gain wholesomeness, we need to cultivate healthy deeds, thoughts, and words. That will contribute to security and stability in our own life and further wholesomeness. Next is to share that wholesomeness with those immediately around us. Going further, we share it with the larger community and the environment. Finally, the best is when we can practice toward liberation from suffering by using wisdom and by helping others attain their own liberation. We help others attain liberation by applying our compassion and by sharing and teaching the Buddhadharma. This is the best kind of wholesomeness.

Recently a woman said to me, "Shifu, you must get my husband to go on a seven-day retreat so that you can use the Buddhadharma to discipline him a little bit."

I asked her, "How about you?"

She said, "Well, I'm not the problem; he's the one who causes all the problems at home."

So I asked her, "You mean you never have vexations?"

She said, "Yes, but it's all because of him, he causes all these problems that give me vexations. That's why you should try to get him to come to practice."

Since I don't know her husband, I cannot verify if what she claims is true. I can say that this woman sees herself as wholesome relative to her husband, but she does not take responsibility for her own vexations and instead attributes them to her husband. In other words, she does not see her own unwholesomeness in the absolute sense. Depending on how we look at it, something that we think is wholesome is actually unwholesome, and vice versa.

I hope this gives you a better understanding of what is wholesome and what is unwholesome. The idea is to enhance diligence by cultivating absolute wholesomeness, which is a mind unmoved by the environment, a mind that remains clear and calm no matter what is happening.

Enhancing the Roots of Mindfulness

We cultivate mindfulness when we practice the Four Foundations of Mindfulness. We should also know that the Four Foundations are based on the Four Noble Truths, which are first, that existence is suffering; second, that the origin of suffering is ignorance; third, that cessation of suffering is possible; and fourth, that the way out of suffering is through the Noble Eightfold Path. Now the seventh noble path is Right Mindfulness, so we can see that practicing mindfulness is there from the beginning of the Buddha's teachings.

Having laid down the roots of mindfulness, how do we enhance them? First, we can contemplate to the point where we understand that body, sensations, mind, and dharmas are impermanent and without self-nature. Sentient beings ordinarily experience phenomena as real and possessing self-identity, and this gives rise to suffering. The Four Foundations of Mindfulness can therefore help us correct our views in accordance with Buddhadharma. This is wisdom, but not necessarily liberation. Although it is possible to realize liberation by practicing the Four Foundations, this is very difficult to achieve. People can hear the Dharma and clearly understand impermanence and ignorance as causes of suffering, but when vexations come up they still suffer. Just cultivating the Four Foundations is not enough. We need to also practice the Four Proper Exertions and the Four Steps to Magical Powers.

Because they are so fundamental for cultivating samadhi, I will go into some additional detail how we practice mindfulness of the body and mindfulness of sensations.

MINDFULNESS OF THE BODY

The first contemplation is to see the body as impure. Some people who are very neat and clean may have difficulty thinking of their bodies as impure. But everyone's body undergoes metabolic changes all day and night, and as a result produces impurities that we excrete as waste. The air we inhale and exhale contains environmental and metabolic impurities. The Chinese use the phrase "smelly skin bag" to refer to the impurity of the body, the idea being that the skin is just a bag holding the collection of bone, flesh, blood, organs, and waste that we call the body. Even if one is more often healthy than unhealthy, could one say that all is well inside the "smelly skin bag"? Is it only when one is sick that this "skin bag" has all sorts of wastes and toxins?

But that is not what I really mean by the impurity of the body. More importantly, the body can also be impure in our attitude toward it. Sentient beings are attached to their body, and have a strong sense of self-love about it. This attachment to the body leads to erroneous views, such as that the self associated with the body is real. The correct view of the body is that it is actually impure in the sense of our attachment to it, and it really should be seen as a tool to use to help others.

The impurity of the body also has to do with conduct. The body's need to fulfill its biological functions leads us to create impure karma. These biological needs are mainly the desire for food, shelter, and sex. Operating with the mind faculty, each of the sense organs—eye, ear, nose, taste, and touch—gives rise to a different kind of desire. Trying to satisfy these desires, we create unwholesome karma.

Therefore we should understand the impurity of the body, first in the sense of physical impurity, and second that the body gives rise to desires through its sense faculties, which results in our creating impure karma. From the perspective of sentient beings, we can say that a healthy body is relatively pure, and a sick body is relatively impure. But do the Buddha and the liberated sages see the body as pure or impure? The answer is that for them the body is neither pure nor impure, but a tool to be used to help sentient beings. We can use the body to constantly pursue our desires, and in this way the body becomes a machine for creating unwholesome karma. Or we can use the body to cultivate virtuous karma: for example, by practicing the Four Foundations of Mindfulness. For buddhas and liberated sages there is no idea of the body being pure or impure. The purity and impurity of the body is only from the perspective of sentient beings. The Buddha merely teaches sentient beings that our belief in the purity of the body is erroneous, and that we need to contemplate its impurity to arrive at a correct view.

One way to contemplate the impurity of the body is through meditation. When we sit in meditation, we experience the body's sensations, how the body feels while sitting. Some of you know that when we meditate, it may feel quite nice in the beginning, but after a while there can be some physical discomfort. You may itch; parts of the body may ache or feel numb; you may feel chilly or hot. Some people get so frustrated with pain in their legs that they feel like cutting them off. These discomforts are especially true if one has been sitting for a long period of time. After a while some people develop an aversion to meditation: "When I don't meditate I feel fine, but when I sit I feel all these discomforts. I might as well give up." At this point, one should remember that the idea of meditation is precisely for one to realize that this body is really not that wonderful. The body is a source of all sorts of discomforts that we don't always recognize. Sometimes it is only when we're doing sitting meditation that we experience things happening in our body at close hand. Through sitting meditation, we can vividly experience that the body is really not such a great thing to have. One can also observe this principle in one's daily life.

Please understand that contemplating the impurity of the body is not in itself negative or pessimistic. Rather, we are talking about the wisdom of recognizing that the body is imperfect and subject to causes and conditions. This wisdom helps us to lessen our attachment to our body, and to gradually eliminate the erroneous view that it is such a great and wonderful thing. If we cling to the idea of the body being pure, then when bad things happen to our body, we will not be able to handle it with a balanced mind, and we will suffer greatly. However, if we understand the fundamental impermanence of the body, then when things happen to it, we will respond with more equanimity and not suffer so much. This is what contemplation of the impurity of the body is about.

On the other hand, one should not take the view that since the body is impure anyway, you may as well do what you want or just kill yourself. That is definitely a wrong view because you are negating the usefulness of the body as a tool for practice. If you now understand the meaning of contemplating the impurity of the body, you have given rise to the virtuous roots. But even if you don't understand, just listening to this talk means you have at least planted virtuous seeds.

MINDFULNESS OF SENSATIONS

As we already know, the second of the Four Foundations is mindfulness of sensations. But to contemplate sensations we need a body. So even though we see the body as being impure, having one is still a positive thing. And what are the sensations that we want to contemplate? They are mental reactions that arise when the sense faculties come into contact with their environment. The sensation of seeing is the mental reaction from the eyes perceiving objects. This is the same when we hear with the ear, smell with the nose, taste with our tongue, or feel with the sense of touch. Sense organs coming into contact with sense objects give rise to sensations. Therefore, the body should be seen positively as a tool for our practice.

In general, we respond to our sensations as unpleasant, pleasant, or neutral (neither pleasant nor unpleasant). We experience sensations as unpleasant when we have pain or discomfort, when we feel dejected, frustrated, or unhappy. We experience sensations as pleasant when we feel joy, happiness, excitement, or some kind of sensual or emotional thrill. However, most of our experience of sensations falls in the area of neither pleasant nor unpleasant, or neutral. It's like going through life as if in a dream, like when you ask someone, "How are things?" and they respond, "Oh, so-so."

In general, these are the three ways we experience sensations. All of them, however, are experiences of the mind. The interesting thing is that even though we talk about sensations being pleasant, unpleasant, or neutral, the Four Foundations teach us to contemplate all sensations as suffering. Why? In truth, understanding sensations as suffering can only be experienced through meditation. To understand why we contemplate sensations as suffering, it would be useful to understand the three aspects of suffering: the suffering of suffering, the suffering of impermanence, and pervasive suffering.

The suffering of suffering is ordinary suffering that we can all recognize—physical pain, illness, separation from a loved one, and so on. From the point of view of having unpleasant sensations, the suffering of suffering is somewhat easy to understand.

The suffering of impermanence is somewhat more subtle than the suffering of suffering, and hence more difficult to understand. For example, when we find pleasure in something, that pleasure may increase or diminish in time. It is subject to change, to impermanence and loss. This means that even the most pleasant experiences are imbued with suffering. There is a Chinese saying that one can experience so much happiness and joy that it is bound to end in disaster. Even the happiest of times flies by quickly. The suffering that comes from the fact that everything is destined to change is called the suffering of impermanence.

Pervasive suffering is due to the fact that we exist as the five aggregates (*skandhas*), of which the fourth, volition, leads to action. Through volition we are prone to pursue desires, so we continuously create conditions for suffering. Although everyone is constantly subject to pervasive suffering, it is only when one is in very deep samadhi that one can most clearly see and understand it. This is because although one may not want the bliss of samadhi to end, it will. Here we see how pervasive suffering is closely associated with the continuous mental activity of the fourth skandha, volition, which governs the formation of desire and intention.

To be truly liberated means one has departed from all three kinds of suffering. That is why it is important to contemplate that all sensations are suffering. What about sensations that are neither pleasant nor unpleasant? What kind of suffering do they correspond to? At the mundane level these neutral sensations make up most of our experience, kind of like a so-so or dream state. But in a very deep samadhi one may also experience no sensations and no thought, only brightness, purity, and clarity of the mind. Even the joy that one may experience in the earlier stages of dhyana has been let go. And so in this deep samadhi there is neither pleasantness nor unpleasantness. This state would correspond to pervasive suffering.

Since suffering is a mental response, we need to understand it from the perspective of how our mind functions. First of all, our thoughts are constantly changing. If you look at a waterfall, you get the impression that it is a steady wall of water. But in fact you are looking at a continuously changing stream composed of drops of water. If you look at it closely, its components in one second are different from its components a second later. This is what it is like in our mind, with changing thoughts constantly flowing through it in a steady stream of impermanence. So pleasant sensations are impermanent, unpleasant sensations are impermanent, and neutral sensations are impermanent as well. All mental activities are impermanent.

Some people think that the teaching of impermanence is negative and pessimistic. If everything is impermanent, they reason, what's the point of doing anything, why take anything seriously? Every baby is going to die someday anyway, so why bother to take care of it? One who thinks this way does not really understand Buddhadharma. When we say that all sensations, including happiness, are impermanent and therefore suffering, what we mean is that we should not get too elated by them. Similarly, we understand that pain is also impermanent, and we are able to have hope that something can be done to alleviate it. With these attitudes we can cultivate virtuous roots. If you understand this, impermanence is not a pessimistic idea.

Most people's daily life revolves around the three kinds of sensations (pleasant, unpleasant, neither pleasant nor unpleasant) as well as the three kinds of suffering (suffering of suffering, suffering of impermanence, pervasive suffering). They mistakenly take the three kinds of sensations and the three kinds of suffering as the self. When we truly understand impermanence, we will give rise to the wisdom that mental and physical phenomena do not have an inherent, independent self. When one can truly contemplate in the fourth foundation of mindfulness that all dharmas are without self, one will gain liberation from the self. But it is important to understand that liberation is not the ultimate realization. With liberation, one has left behind suffering and vexation, but there is still wisdom and compassion to cultivate. When you can completely understand this, you have attained liberation.

Enhancing the Roots of Concentration

The fourth of the Five Roots is the virtuous root of concentration. By "virtuous" we mean that which is wholesome and in accordance with the path of liberation, as well as the path of the bodhisattva.

We can speak of virtue at three levels. At the first level are the wholesome deeds we associate with ordinary morality; at a higher level are the wholesome deeds of one who follows the path of liberation; at the highest level are the wholesome deeds of bodhisattvas practicing for the sake of all sentient beings. At all of these levels, one still cultivates virtuous roots.

The first level of virtue concerns ordinary morality. This consists of the behavior of people who have a good heart, who are willing to help others, and who do not engage in behavior that causes harm to others. They may be wealthy philanthropists; they may be people who don't have much money but give of themselves and their time. These kinds of wholesome deeds are in accordance with the first level of virtue. For the practitioner, the first level of virtue includes upholding the Buddhist precepts. There are two aspects to upholding the precepts: first, not doing things that hurt others; second, doing things that benefit others. For sentient beings practicing at this first level of virtue, their next-life prospects include being reborn in the human or heavenly realms.

At the second level of virtue, in addition to upholding the precepts, we cultivate samadhi and wisdom. Samadhi includes all the methods for practicing meditative concentration. Wisdom means awakening to the true nature of self and suffering and ultimately being enlightened. Together, precepts, samadhi, and wisdom are the three disciplines that make up the path of liberation. I emphasize that samadhi by itself cannot lead to liberation; wisdom is also necessary. However without samadhi, wisdom is very difficult to realize. Because of its emphasis on upholding precepts, the path of liberation includes the virtuous practices of the first level. The difference between ordinary virtue and the virtue of one who is on the path of liberation is that in the latter we do not just uphold the precepts; we also practice samadhi and wisdom.

The third level of virtue is that of the bodhisattva who has vowed to liberate sentient beings. It goes without saying that this includes the virtuous practices of the first two levels. Some people think that the aim of liberating all sentient beings is not practical for them, and that they should realistically just practice for their own liberation: "How can I liberate sentient beings when I haven't even liberated myself?" Others will encourage their family and friends to practice while being lax themselves. These kinds of attitudes are problematic.

There are also practitioners who have practiced for decades and often attend retreats. The interesting thing is that despite their diligence, they have not influenced the people around them as to the benefits of practicing Buddhism. Sometimes their families and friends even think they are odd because they spend so much time meditating. Yesterday when the retreat ended, I told a participant, "Well, you have come to so many retreats; perhaps you can share what you have gained, to influence people around you. Do you have friends that practice the Dharma with you?"

"Yes, Shifu," he said.

"Who?"

"You, Shifu, you and all these people from the Chan Center and the Retreat Center, that's all I need."

We can perhaps say that people like this are cultivating virtue, but not yet at the highest level.

To cultivate the fourth virtuous root of concentration, we need to also cultivate the first three roots—faith, diligence, and mindfulness. We need to have practiced the Four Foundations of Mindfulness, the Four Proper Exertions, and the Four Steps to Magical Powers. These are practices that lead to the generation of samadhi.

What then is samadhi? In general samadhi is the state where the mind is steadily focused on one point and there are no wandering thoughts. There are many levels of samadhi, including some states that are often called samadhi, but are really pre-samadhi states. First there is a feeling of mental pliancy—the mind feels light and at ease. This level can be called *shamatha*, and is characterized by stillness and calm. The next stage is sometimes called neighboring samadhi, where the mind is intensely concentrated, close to one-pointed samadhi but not yet.

While these pre-samadhi and near-samadhi states are useful, the genuine samadhis are the four dhyana levels of the form realm, plus the four dhyana levels of the formless realm [see Glossary]. All these eight levels of samadhi are called worldly samadhi because they are not yet the nonworldly samadhi of liberation, where one attains arhatship. Thus the samadhi of liberation is the ninth level. Nevertheless, one needs to cultivate and transcend worldly samadhi in order to attain the samadhi of liberation. To do this we cultivate the fourth virtuous root, concentration. The nonworldly samadhi that is attained can also be called the samadhi that extinguishes sensation and thought, or the samadhi that extinguishes mental states. In this nonworldly samadhi, one does not attach to the five worldly desires, which are based on the sense faculties. One transcends even the experience of very deep samadhi and no longer attaches to it.

A very important point, therefore, is not to attach to worldly samadhi as liberation. Before and after the time of the Buddha, many religious and philosophical schools had personal liberation as their goal. However, because there were different ideas of liberation, there arose different methods to attain it. Shakyamuni Buddha was learned in the schools and their practices, but arrived at his own understanding of liberation and the way to attain it. He discovered for himself the eight worldly samadhis and the four dhyanas, but he also transcended worldly samadhi and reached the nonworldly samadhi of liberation.

Hearing all this talk about samadhi and its nine levels, some may think, "How does it relate to me? I haven't even really thought about experiencing samadhi." Well, I am telling you about the wealth that you already have in your account, wealth that you can withdraw and use at any time. It's your wealth, not mine. I'm just telling you that it is there. Some of you may not be interested in or feel ready to use this wealth. But to really understand what samadhi is about, you need to experience it yourself. It is not even necessary to achieve very deep samadhi; you only need to experience the samadhi of mental pliancy, of lightness-and-ease. Just getting to that first level would be interesting and beneficial.

I just finished giving a seven-day retreat, and here are some stories that illustrate planting virtuous roots even when one does not attain samadhi. During most of the retreat, one student's mind was kind of scattered and she did not practice very well. But on the afternoon before she had to return to work, she had several hours of very good meditation. The point is that regardless of what happened before, as long as you have some time left, you have a good opportunity to practice.

There was also a practitioner who sat without interruption for more than four hours on the fourth day of the retreat. The whole time, he was clearly aware of what was going on in the Chan Hall. He was aware of sensations, like hearing the sound of the wooden fish [drum] to signal the start of each sitting, and the bell at the end. He was clearly aware of people leaving for lunch and coming back, but all that had nothing to do with him. This is cultivating the virtuous root of concentration.

Then there was a practitioner who didn't ask any questions at all during any of the interviews. After the retreat I asked him how the retreat went.

"It went very well."

I asked him, "In what way was it good?"

He said, "The entire seven days I was either entertaining wandering thoughts or I was drowsy."

For seven days this fellow spent his whole time either entertaining wandering thoughts or being drowsy. So I asked him, "Didn't you find that a waste of time?"

He said, "No, not at all. When I have wandering thoughts or when I'm drowsy, other people do not bother me at all. I still want to come back the next time."

"But is it useful for you now, going back to your daily life?"

"Yes," he said, "for me to stick it out for seven days not being able to talk, smoke, drink alcohol, and for me to obey all the rules, even with drowsiness and wandering thoughts, is something. I have learned patience."

These examples show that even when you do not attain samadhi, you are still practicing and planting virtuous roots. The sutras confirm that when one cultivates samadhi but does not enter it, one still nurtures virtuous roots. At the very least, in cultivating samadhi we become aware that our mind is truly quite scattered, that we do not really have control over it, that it is out of balance. Upon such realization we have an opportunity to stabilize our personality, improve

75

our character, and lessen our internal struggles. Just as important, we will be able to lessen our conflicts with others and the environment.

Even if we do not experience samadhi, when we apply the method in daily life we will not experience so many emotional ups and downs, or be bothered so much by the environment. We gain a greater sense of peace and calmness. There are many benefits in cultivating samadhi even if we do not attain it.

A student of mine witnessed the 2001 terrorist attack at the World Trade Center. During the attack, she couldn't comprehend what was going on. Afterward she was overcome by the horror and was in shock for quite a long time. She was still very much affected by the experience when she came to a seven-day retreat. Toward the end, she told me that even though she still had strong memories of the incident, the retreat helped her to calm and stabilize her mind.

One who cultivates samadhi can maintain a clearer mind when they encounter danger in daily life, and will be less likely to panic. Even if one cannot totally escape danger, if one has a calm and clear mind, the harm one will suffer will likely be less. When we speak of cultivating samadhi to help us in daily life, we are not just referring to sitting practice; we are also talking about mindfulness. This means always being aware of potential problems and crises in daily life. It doesn't mean being constantly worried, but being very mindful of one's conduct. When people say, "Take care, be careful," we intellectually know what that means, but we don't always really follow this advice. To be psychologically prepared means to be aware of danger, to be alert to one's environment and to one's conduct. This way, when problems occur, we are less likely to panic and more likely to lessen the harm that would otherwise occur to ourselves and others.

In situations of danger, many Chinese Buddhists will recite the name of Amitabha Buddha (Namo Amitofo) or of Avalokiteshvara Bodhisattva (Namo Guan Shi Yin Pu Sa). These methods help us to calm our mind and avoid panic, but they also remind us that we still have the buddhas and bodhisattvas to help us. Another method is to focus on your breath, observing it going in and out. Or one can observe the fear in one's own mind. Being aware of our fear, we can tell ourselves that we need to keep our mind clear to handle the problem appropriately. So invoking the buddhas' and bodhisattvas' names or observing one's breath and one's mind can be useful methods.

For some of you, talking about entering samadhi may not sound realistic. Even so, just being able to maintain a calm and stable mind is very useful in daily life. The best way to begin cultivating samadhi is to practice meditation. After you have practiced for a while, then you should attend retreats, beginning with short ones, then eventually going on seven-day or longer retreats. That will be a very good way to develop a calm and stable mind and to cultivate samadhi.

Enhancing the Roots of Wisdom

The fifth virtuous root is wisdom. "Having good karmic roots" is a Chinese phrase to describe someone who has very good innate capacity for practicing Buddhadharma. In the same sense, we can say that those of you who come to these lectures have good wisdom roots. To cultivate wisdom and attain enlightenment, one needs to first hear the Dharma, beginning with the Four Noble Truths. After the Buddha realized complete enlightenment, he gave his first teaching on the Four Noble Truths to his five disciples. This illustrates the Buddha's own experience: first he gave rise to wisdom through cultivation; then he applied that wisdom to helping others.

The Four Noble Truths need to be understood in terms of the three turnings, or stages of realization. The first turning is to hear the Four Noble Truths and understand their meaning. The second turning is to believe in the Four Noble Truths and enter the path of practice. The third turning is to actually realize the Four Noble

Truths through cessation of suffering. At this third turning, suffering and the causes of suffering are extinguished, and one has attained liberation. All that one needs to learn and practice has been learned and practiced. From then on, one does not experience suffering. In other words, one has become an arhat.

The first noble truth says that suffering is a fact of existence. Ordinary people begin the Buddhist path by understanding the reality of suffering. As we have already discussed, there are three aspects of suffering: the suffering of suffering, the suffering of impermanence, and pervasive suffering. It is important to remember them in this order, because those are the stages in which one can understand the reality of suffering. The suffering of suffering is the easiest one to see and understand; it is the suffering you actually can perceive and feel. The suffering of impermanence can best be understood by looking back at one's experiences, and then from logical inference, seeing how the fact that all things change causes suffering. Pervasive suffering is the most subtle, and one cannot truly see it until one experiences very deep samadhi.

Most people cannot truly admit or understand the level and extent of suffering in their lives. It is difficult to even think of wanting to depart from suffering, much less practicing to depart from suffering. For example, insects can live without knowing about suffering or the need to depart from suffering. Without any real safety or security they just go on living, not thinking about suffering at all. Human beings, however, do experience and know the reality of suffering. But ordinarily, people have no idea about the reality of pervasive suffering. That comes from the wisdom of the Buddha, who taught it to us in the first noble truth of the existence of suffering.

The second noble truth says that the cause of suffering is the karma we create through our deeds, thoughts, and words. Karma is the law of cause and effect, and when we create karma we are creating the causes of suffering. Suffering is the fruit of karma. Most people are aware of suffering when it comes to fruition, but they are not aware of the moment when they are planting the seeds of future suffering. At the time they are doing unwholesome deeds, they might actually be quite happy and proud of what they are doing.

Through our actions, words, and thoughts, we create different kinds of karma. People cannot read our mind, nor can we read other people's minds, but we can see people's actions and hear their words. Nevertheless, what people do and say has its origins in what they think. If someone has an unwholesome thought but does not carry it out, does that create karma? Obviously, just thinking is not as bad as doing or saying. Therefore, we distinguish between having an unwholesome thought and actually doing and saying something unwholesome.

For example, you are desperate for money and the thought of stealing occurs to you. That is an unwholesome thought, but if it just remains a thought, then that is just thinking. However, if in addition to the thought of stealing money you begin to plan how you would do it, then even if you don't carry out the plan, an intention has been formed. This kind of mental karma is called the karma of effective thinking.

The karma of effective thinking is not necessarily negative. For example, you heard that there was going to be a lecture at the Chan Center on the Five Roots and the Five Powers, and that aroused your interest. You followed up on your thought and decided, "I ought to go and check it out." Now you are here, and I say that your being here shows that you have roots of wisdom. This is another example of the karma of effective thinking.

So there is unwholesome karma and wholesome karma. Within wholesome karma, we have karma without outflows and karma with outflows. Karma without outflows refers to practicing in order to liberate oneself from vexations and to depart from suffering. In creating wholesome karma without outflows, we earn merits for a better life in this world or a better rebirth, such as being reborn in the heavenly realm. Wholesome karma with outflows refers to helping others and cultivating good interactions with other people.

Within both karma with outflows and karma without outflows, there is collective karma and individual karma. When people live in the same environment, think and influence each other in the same ways, then they also act in similar ways. This creates a shared collective karma. However, people living within a group still have their own personalities, preferences, and habits. Therefore they create individual karma. Even identical twins will create different karma.

So within karma without outflows, there is still collective as well as individual karma. For instance, practitioners have in common their belief in the law of causes and conditions, in the law of cause and effect, and the law of karma; they believe as well in the three disciplines of upholding the precepts, and in cultivating samadhi and wisdom. This is the collective karma within karma without outflows. But practitioners may also vary in their approach and emphasis. There are those cultivating the path of a *shravaka*, and there are those who choose the path of a bodhisattva. Some who choose the bodhisattva path may emphasize practicing charity (*dana*), while some may emphasize the study of Buddhadharma, or the cultivation of supernormal powers. These choices create individual wholesome karma without outflows.

When we understand how collective as well as individual karma come about, then we begin to understand why people living in the same era and the same society have different life conditions. Some people enjoy material wealth and comfort, have a lot of friends, and accomplish everything easily. Others live in poverty, have few friends, and have a life full of obstacles. There are people who enjoy good health and those who have very poor health. All these things result from collective and individual karma. If one cannot see these differences from the perspective of karma, one may be tempted to complain about how bad one's life is compared to others. There is a Chinese saying that goes, "Why is this happening to me? Heaven must be blind." I don't know if Westerners tend to blame someone else for their problems, but if we understand that our experience is the result of all kinds of unwholesome and wholesome karma, then we may be less likely to blame God or heaven for our misfortune.

So there is the karma of thinking and the karma of effective thinking, and either can be wholesome and unwholesome. An example of the wholesome karma of thinking and the wholesome karma of effective thinking is to vow to help sentient beings. We don't just make this vow once; we make it over and over, and we also go about helping sentient beings. We cannot do everything in this life, so we also vow to continue in the next life. Because of such vows we may even encounter misfortune. Compassionate vows made in a past life may even result in dire circumstances in this life, in which one fulfills one's vow by sacrificing their life for others.

What people may see as negative circumstances are really the results of virtuous roots planted by vowing to help sentient beings. For example, victims of terrorist attacks can see their suffering as a result of having vowed to offer themselves for the sake of eliminating terrorism and promoting peace. In this way we can make sense of the suffering of these victims.

When we cultivate karma without outflows, we are on the path toward the cessation of suffering. As for wholesome and unwholesome karma, the idea is simply to refrain from creating unwholesome karma and to create only wholesome karma. To cultivate the path toward liberation, we start with the Four Foundations of Mindfulness, and then go to the Four Proper Exertions, then to the Four Steps to Magical Powers, then to the Five Roots and the Five Powers, then to the Seven Factors of Enlightenment, and all the way to the Noble Eightfold Path. That makes up the Thirty-seven Aids to Enlightenment. However, it is not necessary to practice in this order. You can also try to understand and practice the Four Noble Truths as much as possible. That way, you will be practicing along the path of sudden enlightenment.

I sometimes refer to stages of practice in terms of sage and saint. On the level of a sage, one's practice is certainly advanced. For example, a sage is one who already practices the Four Steps to Magical Powers, but until one has cultivated the Five Roots and the Five Powers we cannot speak of sainthood. Thus the difference between sage and saint is that the former has cultivated samadhi, but the latter has also cultivated the roots of wisdom.

Cultivating the roots of wisdom encompasses many levels, but it begins with the initial aspiration to follow the Path. For example, we have a bodhisattva who came here eight years ago, who wasn't here all that time but showed up today to take refuge. Does this bodhisattva have roots of wisdom? Of course he does. Another person here today comes every week. Does he also have roots of wisdom? Of course he does.

Some may think that the Thirty-seven Aids to Enlightenment are too complicated and a lot of trouble. You begin with the Four Foundations of Mindfulness, and then take up the Four Proper Exertions, and then the Four Steps to Magical Powers. After that you practice the Five Roots and the Five Powers, then the Seven Factors of Enlightenment, and then finally the Noble Eightfold Path. That sounds like a lot of stages. On the other hand, a shravaka, someone who has very deep roots of wisdom, can attain enlightenment upon hearing just a few words of Dharma. The shravaka can then go on to attain all four fruition levels of the arhat, ultimately entering nirvana. However, the appearance of a shravaka is a very rare occurrence.

The third noble truth says that while suffering is a fact of existence, and that we are the cause of our own suffering, it is possible to bring suffering to cessation. The fourth noble truth tells us that the way to bring suffering to cessation is through following the Noble Eightfold Path. Following the Path means purifying one's conduct, thought, and speech. In general, this means refraining from unwholesomeness and cultivating wholesomeness. Through these means one can bring about the cessation of suffering. By the end of the Buddha's first sermon, one of the monks was fully liberated; that is, he became an arhat. After the Buddha gave the teaching a second and third time, the remaining monks were at least enlightened to their true self-nature. Just hearing the teaching three times, they all became enlightened. So if you hear or think that sudden enlightenment was invented by Chinese Chan, please remember that five monks became enlightened after hearing the Buddha's very first teachings. Does this sound easy? Not really. What the monks realized was only possible because they had very deep roots of wisdom and had been practicing hard for a long time.

When you hear the Buddhadharma and can accept its teachings, you are already planting your own roots of wisdom. Whether that will allow you to become enlightened depends on how strong and deep those roots are. You can't really know the depth of your own roots from your current experience. You may think because you are not yet enlightened that you don't have wisdom roots. That is not necessarily true. The fact that you are here to listen to the Dharma means that you do have wisdom roots.

5

THE SEVEN FACTORS
OF ENLIGHTENMENT

As a topic the Seven Factors of Enlightenment would be foreign to most people, yet a lot of people have come here to hear me talk about it. It seems that the more exotic the topic, the more interest there is in it. This probably has to do with the word "enlightenment," which is always very enticing to people. Actually, it *is* possible to attain enlightenment. That is in fact what happened to Shakyamuni Buddha. If enlightenment were not possible, what would be the point of teaching the Dharma?

The Arya-Sarvastivada school of early Buddhism considered the Thirty-seven Aids to Enlightenment to be the gist of the practice toward liberation. Having completed the Thirty-seven Aids, one would become an arhat. However, when I discuss the Thirty-seven Aids, I also talk about how they are practiced in the Mahayana tradition. My perspective on how they are practiced in the Chan tradition will also differ somewhat from other traditions.

Since most Chan masters teach sudden enlightenment, they do not talk much about the Thirty-seven Aids, which are considered gradual methods. However, I do teach gradual methods as the foundation for practice toward sudden enlightenment. For those capable of realizing sudden enlightenment, that is wonderful and they can dispense with the gradual methods. However, those for whom sudden enlightenment is not that feasible can practice gradual methods as a foundation for the sudden methods.

Therefore when I speak of the Thirty-seven Aids, it is in the context of both the Hinayana path of the shravaka and the Mahayana path of the bodhisattva. The difference between the two paths is basically one of attitude and emphasis. Although we often think of Chan as a method for sudden enlightenment, it indeed progresses in stages. In this respect, Chan agrees with the gradual approach of the Thirty-seven Aids. For example, prior to the Four Foundations we practice the Five Methods of Stilling the Mind to collect the scattered mind into one that is stable and unified. After the Five Methods, one is ready to practice the Four Foundations. Within each group the practices can also be seen as sequential. For example, in the Four Foundations, mindfulness of body precedes mindfulness of sensations, and so on. As we practice the Thirty-seven Aids we continuously make progress toward liberation. By the time we get to the Seven Factors of Enlightenment, we should be quite far along the path, though not yet liberated.

The Sanskrit term for the Seven Factors of Enlightenment is *sapta-bodhyanga,* where *sapta* means "seven," *bodhi* means "enlightenment," and *anga* means "factor" or "item." Each group in the Thirty-seven Aids has a distinct name, but in fact all thirty-seven aids can be called *bodhyanga* since they are all factors toward enlightenment. The Seven Factors of Enlightenment are called that because after completing their cultivation, one should be enlightened. In Chinese translations of the sutras, *sapta-bodhyanga* is rendered in various ways. I will not dwell on this, except to make you aware that there are differences in how the term is translated in Chinese.

The Seven Factors are (1) *mindfulness* in both mental and physical activities; (2) *discernment* between dharmas (as real or illusory); (3) *diligence,* or perseverance; (4) *joy,* or rapture; (5) *lightness-and-*

ease, or tranquility; (6) *concentration;* and (7) *equanimity,* meaning freedom from discrimination or dualistic thinking.

The seven groups of practices in the Thirty-seven Aids are sequential and within each group, the practices are also considered sequential. So, with the Seven Factors of Enlightenment, mindfulness leads to discernment, which leads to diligence, which leads to joy, and so on. However, their sequential nature does not mean that going from one factor to the next, one leaves behind the others. As one makes progress the factors coexist; indeed, they energize one to proceed to the next. For example, without joy as well as lightness-and-ease, it would be difficult to penetrate deeply the practice of concentration.

Mindfulness

Cultivating mindfulness essentially means practicing the Four Foundations of Mindfulness: mindfulness of the body, mindfulness of sensations, mindfulness of mind, and depending on one's tradition, mindfulness of causes and conditions or mindfulness of the buddhas. We should also remember at this point that the purpose of practicing the Four Foundations is to cultivate wisdom. Mindfulness of the body has three aspects: mindfulness of the inner body, mindfulness of the outer body, and mindfulness of the inner-and-outer body. The inner body refers to the internal organs—heart, liver, bodily fluids, and so on. The outer body refers to the sense organs—eye, ear, nose, tongue, and touch; specifically, how the body responds to the environment. The inner-and-outer body refers to the integration of the inner and the outer body. In practicing mindfulness of the body, we pay attention to all three aspects.

We cultivate mindfulness of the body to see the body as it really is, to not be so attached to it. We often fret and worry about every little thing that happens to our body. Some people love their body, some hate it, but both attitudes reveal overattachment to the body as a source of vexations. Being mindful of the body, we understand that it is constantly undergoing change and that things will happen to it. This helps us let go of overattachment to the body and thus not create so much vexation.

When we think of our body, we are usually concerned with issues like comfort or discomfort, health or sickness, whether we are attractive or ugly, and so on. Preoccupied by such thoughts, we rarely see our body objectively; instead we usually see the body as "mine," and having this or that state or quality: "I'm good-looking" or "I'm ugly." When we can look at the body more objectively, we will be practicing mindfulness of the body.

Mindfulness of sensations means being aware of one's sensory perceptions, whether they are pleasant, unpleasant, or neutral. For example, when we are comfortable, we are aware of a pleasant feeling; when we are uncomfortable, we are aware of an unpleasant feeling, and when we are neither comfortable nor uncomfortable, we are aware of that. In other words, mindfulness of sensations means being aware of your sensations at the very moment you experience them. For example, right now are your sensations pleasant, unpleasant, or neither pleasant nor unpleasant?

Mindfulness of the mind is being aware of how we mentally react to sensations. When we feel pleasure, we crave for more or fear that we will lose it; when we feel discomfort, we resent it and want to get rid of it. We are excited about a happy experience, but get frustrated when we encounter misfortune. We thus have greed on the one hand and aversion on the other. And when our experience is neither pleasant nor unpleasant, we get bored or lethargic. With all these vexations, it is easy to be confused about what we really want in life. So mindfulness of the mind means to be aware of how we react to our experiences.

Mindfulness of dharmas is being attentive to whether our mental objects—ideas, concepts, symbols, language, feelings—are wholesome or unwholesome, beneficial or harmful. Just as we need to be mindful of the body, of sensations, and of our mental reactions to sensations, we need to be very clear about how our mental processes create wholesome as well as unwholesome results.

How can we practice mindfulness in daily life? Let me give you an example of mindfulness of the body in daily life. Recently a lady said to me, "Shifu, I need to have surgery and I am really scared."

"What are you afraid of?" I asked.

"First I'm afraid of the pain, second I'm afraid I'll die from the surgery."

I told her, "The more afraid you are of the pain, the more pain you're going to feel. Tell yourself that your body is being treated by your doctor and you are just witnessing it."

Later she told me that because she was under local anesthesia she could observe the surgery and was not afraid. She said, "What I saw was just the doctor performing surgery on a body." This lady was practicing mindfulness of the body.

If you succeed in contemplating the body, you will also be very clear about your sensations. If you succeed in contemplating sensations, you will be very clear about your mental activities. And if you can do that, you will be able to contemplate dharmas very clearly, to see what's going on clearly. And this is how we cultivate the Four Foundations of Mindfulness.

Discernment

Discernment means distinguishing real from illusory dharmas. It also means understanding the difference between the wholesome and the unwholesome. If one understands the difference, one will move toward wholesomeness and begin to depart from vexations. And once we depart from vexations we also move toward wisdom, away from hatred and toward compassion. With the cultivation of discernment, we move forward on the path of liberation, which is to say, of wisdom and compassion.

What then is real as opposed to illusory? Without practicing the Four Foundations of Mindfulness, it can be difficult to understand the distinction. For example, if one sees the body as existing independently, or as being real, that would be illusory and unwholesome. Similarly, when we contemplate sensations we understand that whether they are pleasant or unpleasant, they are relative and not absolute. In a good mood even a minor thing can seem pleasant, whereas in a bad mood something supposedly pleasant can seem unpleasant. Through contemplation we can thus see that sensations do not have absolute and inherent qualities.

There was a young man who was attracted to a young woman who completely ignored him. One time he approached her and was perhaps a little too fresh, and she slapped him in the face. When he felt the slap, the young man was overjoyed. Can you relate to this? What was going on?

Student: She ignored him before, but when she slapped him she was finally paying attention. So that made him happy.

Sheng Yen: That's right. This story shows the relative nature of sensations. In this case being slapped in the face was a pleasant sensation for this young man.

Similarly, when we contemplate the mind we can see that its contents have no absolute quality, but are relative to events and transient. When we contemplate mental dharmas, we see that they are empty of self. We will see therefore that being mindful of body, sensations, mind, and dharmas is wholesome, and discerning the real from the illusory is wisdom. Through contemplating the four kinds of mindfulness, we realize that all phenomena are impermanent and therefore empty. This wisdom allows one to know absolute truth and relative truth. Absolute truth refers to the emptiness of dharmas and the law of causes and conditions, while relative truth refers to the transient phenomena of daily life. With discernment, we will know the difference between wisdom and vexation.

Diligence

Without acquiring some wisdom and knowing true Dharma from false Dharma, trying to practice with great diligence may be like a blind person riding a blind horse. Two dangers of practicing blindly like this are that first, one may fall into the error of believing incorrect Dharma, and second, one may practice incorrect methods. Therefore to truly practice with diligence, one should be guided by a teacher who has the correct understanding of Dharma and who practices the proper methods. Otherwise, without a qualified teacher one would not know how to deal with unusual physical or mental states they may encounter.

How do you know if the teacher is teaching the proper Dharma? First, consider whether the teacher has a correct understanding of the key concepts of Buddhism. This means the teacher should exhibit a clear understanding and acceptance of the law of cause and effect. This teacher would not use their position to benefit himself or herself, and would not do unwholesome deeds because they would know that there would be retribution through karma. They would know very clearly that to receive wholesome results, one ought to engage in wholesome deeds.

A good teacher of Buddhism also needs to understand the law of conditioned arising, which states that all things exist as a coming together of myriad causes and conditions, and therefore everything is impermanent, without an inherent self. Understanding phenomena in this manner means that one possesses basic Buddhist wisdom. A student can thus use their own understanding of karma and the law of causes and conditions to evaluate whether the teacher or method is in accordance with correct Dharma. A teacher who truly practices according to these laws is a good teacher; if a method encompasses these two ideas, it is a good method.

To practice with diligence we therefore need to distinguish between proper Dharma and erroneous views, and we need teachers who know the difference. What is the proper Dharma? The Thirty-seven Aids to Enlightenment are the proper Dharma and the proper methods of practice. Understanding these proper methods, one can then practice diligently. What is diligent practice? It is to practice the Four Proper Exertions. If it seems like we are going back to the Four Proper Exertions again, that is correct. This time, however, we are talking about the Four Proper Exertions in the context of the Seven Factors of Enlightenment.

Here is how to understand this process. To review, the first five groups are the Four Foundations of Mindfulness, the Four Proper Exertions, the Four Steps to Magical Powers, the Five Roots, and the Five Powers. These five groups are really about cultivating samadhi power as you make progress. When we begin to practice, our samadhi power is relatively weak, so we need to build a solid foundation. Then as our samadhi power deepens we move to the next stage, but we also go back to the foundation methods to improve our contemplation. Over time, this process will allow one to advance one's power of samadhi. In other words, making progress is not a simple linear process; as you make progress you also revisit the foundation methods.

It is not correct to think that you must go through all the Thirty-seven Aids to attain liberation. Indeed, if one has very sharp virtuous roots, one can attain liberation just by practicing the Four Foundations of Mindfulness. And if that is just not quite enough to get one there, one can add the next step, the Four Proper Exertions. And if that's still not enough, then one can practice the Four Steps to Magical Powers, and that can be enough for some. And if one is not able to attain liberation by practicing those three groups, one can cultivate the Five Roots and the Five Powers. And if that still does not do it, one will need to cultivate the Seven Factors of Enlightenment. In fact, the Seven Factors of Enlightenment are

THE SEVEN FACTORS OF ENLIGHTENMENT

themselves adequate to attain liberation, because they are seven methods for cultivating bodhi. If the cultivation of the Seven Factors of Enlightenment is still not enough for liberation, then one ends up with the Noble Eightfold Path as well.

Getting enlightened is not like weight lifting where you keep lifting heavier and heavier weights. Some people can only lift ten pounds while others can lift several hundred pounds. It is kind of the opposite with the Path. Those who have the most virtuous roots need to take fewer steps and to hear less Dharma to attain liberation. If you need to practice all seven groups to be liberated, that is because you don't have quite adequate virtuous roots under your belt. So if you have heard all the previous lectures and are still here listening to this talk about the Seven Factors of Enlightenment, you must come back for the lectures on the Noble Eightfold Path. [*Laughter*]

Whether you are already enlightened or have poor virtuous roots, it is still useful to hear the Thirty-seven Aids explained. The more one hears the Dharma, the more virtuous roots one will develop. Even if one did not practice before hearing the Dharma, afterward one will think more of the need for practice. So it is still beneficial for you to listen to Dharma and still useful for me to teach it.

To repeat, diligence actually refers to the Four Proper Exertions. This means first, avoiding new unwholesome practices; second, cutting off existing unwholesome practices; third, beginning new wholesome practices; and fourth, continuing existing wholesome practices. This is what diligence means.

For example, one has vowed to practice the Dharma, and one has also vowed to cut off unwholesome behavior and unwholesome speech. Although that is good, one may not yet be able to avoid unwholesome thoughts. So the practice of the Four Proper Exertions is to also vow to cut off unwholesome thoughts.

To take this practice to a deeper level, you not only vow to avoid unwholesome behavior, you also vow to engage in new wholesome behavior. We are usually happy to be recognized and rewarded when we do good things, but that is not good enough because the expectation of praise or reward is itself a vexation. So one goes further and makes this vow: "From now on, I will not expect any reward from wholesome behavior." That would be a deeper level of practicing diligence.

On the path to enlightenment, exertion means practicing with great perseverance and great patience, and being continuously engaged. Some may misunderstand this to mean going full force and forgetting about daily life. Far from being proper exertion, that is more like a demonic kind of practice. Rather, proper exertion is like a small stream flowing without pause—not too tense and not too lax. When you are too tense, it is possible to fall into a demonic state where you generate unwholesome thoughts and attitudes. When you are too lax, you will not be really engaged; you will be like a deflated balloon, not able to generate any power. Proper exertion, therefore, is being ceaselessly engaged in the practice—not too tense, not too lax, with great perseverance and patience.

This morning I asked my attendant to cook some millet for me. The millet that she uses sometimes still has husks that get stuck between my teeth. So I asked her to remove the grains with husks before cooking the millet. She said, "Shifu, it's very hard to find the ones with husks." I started showing her how to do it, and I would pick one out and say, "See, this is one with a husk." I picked up another one, then another one, one by one. I was just doing this in a very concentrated manner, until my attendant said, "Shifu, it's almost time for your lecture!" And then I realized that an hour and a half had passed! It was very joyful for me to do this and I did not see it as a chore. As far as I was concerned, I was picking out pearls.

Joy

The key to diligence is great patience, without any sense of great like or dislike about what one is doing, without thinking of gain and loss. If you practice this way, inevitably joy will arise. This joy is not the mundane kind of joy we are all familiar with, but the joy that comes from hearing and living the Dharma. Therefore we also call it Dharma joy. Before encountering the Dharma, we have a lot of erroneous views; we are at war with ourselves, experiencing struggle, conflict, and contradiction; we also have external conflicts. After hearing the Dharma, we understand the law of cause and effect, or karma. We also understand the law of causes and conditions, which says that things happen according to the myriad underlying conditions that exist at any given time. Because of this conditioned arising together, everything is in flux, everything is impermanent, empty, and without inherent self. Upon hearing such a teaching, one should feel joy.

Confucius said that if we hear a good teaching in the morning, we should be ready to die in the evening. Hearing the Dharma is like the thrill you feel when you hear something that brings you to full alertness; you feel the lifting of a heavy burden that you have been carrying for a long time: "Before this, I was so vexed because I was looking at things the wrong way, but now I see the world with a different attitude. I can finally let go of this burden." Do you experience joy when you hear the Dharma? You must to some extent, otherwise why would you be foolish enough to come here on a Sunday to hear me talk? [*Laughter*]

In addition to the joy of hearing the Dharma, there is the joy of practicing meditation. When we cultivate dhyana, we attain stability, peacefulness, and calmness of mind, and we feel Dharma joy. This kind of Dharma joy is not some kind of excitement, but a deeper feeling of inner calm that is not affected by the environment: "I'm just here enjoying this moment of peace and quiet." I believe many of you have experienced this Dharma joy at least to some degree. If you have not and you still come to my retreats, then that is pretty foolish.

Several Tibetan lamas live in exile at our Dharma Drum Mountain temple in Taiwan. Even though they have lost their country, the lamas are always joyful. Many lay practitioners at the temple don't understand this. They ask the lamas, "How is it that you are always so happy after losing your country?" The lamas say, "The loss of our country has been painful, but because we still have the Buddhadharma, we are happy." These lamas are joyful because they are always with the Dharma, living it and teaching it. It is precisely because they live in accordance with the Dharma that monks and nuns are happy. I myself always feel Dharma joy. I hope that you will apply the Seven Factors of Enlightenment in your own life and be immersed in Dharma joy as well.

Lightness-and-Ease

After the experience of Dharma joy, lightness-and-ease, or tranquility, will arise as well. This means being free of the passions of body and mind. Lightness-and-ease is a deeper and subtler realization than Dharma joy, which can be coarse or fine. With Dharma joy there is still much movement of the mind: "Oh, this is so joyful!" That would be a coarser kind of Dharma joy. At a finer level, there is quietude in Dharma joy and one feels lightness in the body, but still lacks the mental pliancy of lightness-and-ease. With mental pliancy, body and mind are unified and one no longer worries about either; one is no longer preoccupied with the body and its sensations, whether it feels light or heavy, even whether it's there, and one is not aware of having any vexations of the mind.

While practicing, some people become aware that they no longer feel sensations, but then they become excited about this: "My body has disappeared; I no longer feel it. That is amazing." This means that one is experiencing lightness of the body, but since the mind takes note of it, some coarseness is still there. In real mental pliancy, even though the body feels weightless, one has no thought of whether the body or the mind is there. When true mental pliancy happens, everything is very easy, smooth, and comfortable. One is sitting there and the wind blows, but one has no notion that they are separate from the wind. The sounds of the environment, my talking, they are all the same. Everything is very harmonious— body, mind, and universe are one. But please do not mistake mental pliancy as just being extremely relaxed and having no vexations. That is a good stage where grosser thoughts and sensations are absent, but it is only when one has unified mind, body, and the environment that one has arrived at lightness-and-ease. At this point one is ready to practice the sixth factor of enlightenment— concentration, or samadhi.

Concentration

In Buddhist practice, there are nine levels of samadhi—the first eight constitute worldly samadhi, while the ninth is called nonworldly samadhi. The first samadhi level is the stage of lightness-and-ease. This is also equivalent to the first dhyana level. One proceeds by stages to the fourth dhyana level, and further on until one reaches the eighth level, which is the deepest level of worldly samadhi. Nonworldly samadhi, the ninth samadhi stage, is referred to in Chan as "sudden enlightenment." It is so called because at the moment of realization, one's worldview is suddenly transformed from one that is upside down, one that is ruled by suffering and vexation, to one in which one's bondage to vexation and suffering is released.

The sutras define samadhi as the state where the mind becomes single-pointed and is totally present. It may sound arduous to start with the first factor of mindfulness and diligently work all the way to the sixth factor of concentration. In reality, all it takes is a change in one's attitude, and it is possible in an instant to experience lightness-and-ease. And if the experience is deep, your mind would become very stable and very peaceful. That would be samadhi. On the other hand, as you hear this lecture, if your mind is totally in the present moment, focused on hearing the Dharma, with no thoughts of good or bad, right or wrong, free of wandering thoughts—that too would be samadhi.

So there are two ways of experiencing samadhi. One comes from changing your attitude, where a turn of thought suddenly allows you to experience samadhi. The other kind comes from the step-by-step cultivation through the four dhyanas and eight levels of samadhi. The second way of samadhi is the deeper way. To put it in mundane terms, the first can be likened to being knocked unconscious, and then waking up and not realizing what happened to you. The second is like falling into a very deep sleep without dreams, and then waking up a few hours later and not realizing you had even been asleep.

You may wonder, "Why should I work so hard cultivating samadhi? I may as well get hit on the head or just go to sleep." The difference is that after regaining consciousness or waking from sleep, one would not experience lightness-and-ease. You would probably be just as prone to irritation as before, and you would probably be subject to the same seductions and distractions. Your character would probably be the same. By contrast, after deep samadhi one will feel great peace of mind and joy. Afterward one would be less likely to respond to negative stimuli or challenges than before.

Equanimity

The seventh factor of enlightenment is equanimity, in Sanskrit *upeksha*, which literally means "not taking notice." We saw that the fifth factor, lightness-and-ease, was a very enjoyable and comfortable feeling—the body is relaxed, without tension, and the mind is settled, without any vexations. But there is always a temptation to become attached to this feeling, to want to remain in it forever because it is so blissful. If one does this, one is like a rock soaking in a pool of water, not doing anything useful. Therefore one needs to practice equanimity, or not taking notice.

As we said, experiencing deep samadhi is very joyful. The fourth factor of joy, the fifth factor of lightness-and-ease, and the sixth factor of concentration are blissful experiences that can emerge from practice. But attaching to such experiences is not proper Buddhist practice. We practice Buddhism to alleviate suffering, but it is also important to be free from attachments to joy as well.

Letting go of joy does not mean that we do not welcome happiness, but rather that we do not crave it, and when we experience it we do not cling to it. Through this practice we will know that there is not one single experience that is permanent, that all things are transitory and thus impermanent and empty. Letting go is cultivating the wisdom of emptiness, an essential condition for liberation.

Conditions for Practicing the Seven Factors

The early Pali scriptures, the *agamas*, speak of three aspects to the practice of the Seven Factors of Enlightenment: first, the conditions that should exist to begin the practice; second, how to practice the factors; and third, how to use the functions and merits gained from the practice. Four important conditions to have for practicing the Seven Factors are virtuous roots, faith in the Dharma, right view, and diligence. I will discuss these and then discuss further guidelines for practice.

VIRTUOUS ROOTS

The first important condition for practicing the Seven Factors is to have virtuous roots. Having virtuous roots and encountering people with wisdom, you should then use every chance to learn Dharma and cultivate faith. This will give you the correct views to guide your conduct in accordance with the Seven Factors of Enlightenment. You also need the right wisdom to do as the Buddha taught, and you need to always protect the six senses. The best way to meet these conditions is to practice the Four Foundations of Mindfulness. The teachings and methods of Buddhadharma are there to guide you, but cultivation is your own responsibility. If you follow this principle you will find freedom from vexation, confusion, and struggle, and you will eventually attain liberation.

Who among you does not have virtuous roots? You may think you lack virtuous roots because you have vexations. If that is so, why are you here today? Clearly, having virtuous roots gave you the desire and willingness to hear the Dharma and be near people with wisdom. Or your being here may be due to causes and conditions. For example, by chance you hear on the radio a discussion on Buddhism that makes sense, and you want to learn more. After looking into it, you end up at a Dharma center. Whether you are here by intention or because of causes and conditions, it was due to your virtuous roots. Either way brings you closer to the Dharma and people with wisdom.

Outside this Chan Center is a bus stop. This place is a little exotic looking, and sometimes people waiting for the bus are curious. They ring our bell; we invite them in, give them some literature, and let them look around. We actually have had people come back to hear a lecture or participate in activities.

Do the people who come in here out of curiosity have virtuous roots? Yes, we can say they do. What are virtuous roots then? They have to do either with having connected with Buddhadharma in the past, or having an outlook that corresponds to what Buddhism teaches. So when causes and conditions ripen, it is not too hard for such people to connect with the Dharma.

What I call "people with wisdom" is often translated in the

sutras as "learned friends." These are people with whom we interact on a level that is beneficial in the Dharma sense, to either or both parties. Therefore those who want to practice the Seven Factors of Enlightenment should have learned friends to help them. Should we remain friends with those who are not beneficial to us? Some feel that if they befriend someone who behaves unwholesomely, they can change them for the better. If that is so, there is no need to discriminate against them. This is a correct view, but it really depends on what kind of person you are. If you can befriend unwholesome people without being affected yourself, that's fine; otherwise it can be a problem. You may intend to deliver sentient beings, but if you are not careful you can end up being delivered yourself, but to the wrong place. [*Laughter*]

You may want to be wary of friends who are not benevolent, but when such people are in need you should still help them. On the other hand, you also need learned friends with whom you can learn Buddhadharma and cultivate wisdom and compassion. But what are wisdom and compassion? The answer is rather simple. When you give rise to vexation and suffering within yourself or through the environment, that is lacking wisdom; when you cause suffering to others, that is lacking compassion. Now turn that around: when you do not cause vexation and suffering to yourself, that is wisdom; when you do not cause vexation and suffering to others, that is compassion.

FAITH IN THE DHARMA

After you have learned something of the Dharma, you give rise to the pure faith that the teachings are useful for yourself and also for others. Then you also have to remind yourself often to use the teachings in your actions. This is the second important condition for practicing the Seven Factors of Enlightenment.

A disciple asked me to help him with his severe headaches.

After he practiced meditation for a while, his headaches went away. After that his faith in Buddhadharma became rock solid. He also served as my translator for twenty years. Another example is a minister who just wanted to learn meditation but not the Dharma. Later on he brought his wife along, and after two meditation classes her insomnia was cured. After that she became a Buddhist. They had an interesting situation—a Christian minister with a Buddhist wife. These things happen not because I have special powers, but because people have the virtuous roots to encounter the Buddhadharma and receive its teachings. Actually, when people complain to me about their headaches, I tell them, "Well, I have headaches too." [*Laughter*]

Faith in the Dharma can arise two ways: first, when Buddhism makes sense to you, and second, when you can apply it to your daily life. Because it is logical, you have faith in it, and because it is useful, you will remember to use it. I know a couple who learned at the same time that they both had cancer, as if they had planned it. It was a very sad thing, but these people also have very virtuous roots. Using the teachings of Dharma, I encouraged them to have faith in themselves and to make vows. Eventually they recovered their health. They are also dedicated volunteers at the Chan Center. These people's virtuous roots allowed them to be close to learned friends, allowed them to practice the Dharma, and as a result they have a pure faith in the teachings.

RIGHT VIEW

In describing the conditions for practicing the Seven Factors, the Hinayana scriptures say, "After one has heard the wondrous Dharma, and one's body has the right posture, and one's mind has the right thought, one can then practice the Seven Factors of Enlightenment step-by-step." "After one has heard the wondrous Dharma" refers to hearing any correct teaching of the Dharma, and thus acquiring the right view. For example, even though I am not really lecturing on a particular sutra, what I am saying comes from the sutras. Therefore any of the true teachings of the Buddha is "wondrous Dharma." Thus the third condition for practicing the Seven Factors is right view, or right wisdom. Right view means living with one's thoughts always in accordance with Dharma; right wisdom means living without vexations. The ability to do so comes from constantly applying the methods to one's daily life.

DILIGENCE

If one has the right view, as the sutras say, "One can then practice the Seven Factors of Enlightenment step-by-step." One proceeds step-by-step, starting with mindfulness, then to discernment, moving on to diligence, then to joy, to lightness-and-ease, then concentration (samadhi), and finally equanimity. This is diligence, the fourth condition for practicing the Seven Factors. This does not mean knowing any particular teaching, but knowing what one needs to do, or stop doing, in order to practice. With right view, one will give rise to the factors that have not yet arisen, and keep cultivating the factors that have already arisen. Right view gives rise to diligence, and diligence means practicing the Four Proper Exertions.

How to Practice the Seven Factors of Enlightenment

Having established the proper conditions for practicing the Seven Factors, one is still in an embryonic stage, so to speak. To continue to grow in the practice, it is necessary to abide by some important guidelines.

PROTECTING THE SIX SENSE FACULTIES

After having right view and right wisdom, one still needs to constantly protect the sense faculties of eye, ear, nose, tongue, body, and mind. To protect the senses means keeping them pure, not allowing them to fall into temptation or be defiled. Difficult as that may be, you need to constantly protect your six senses. Like my eyeglasses— the only way I keep them free of dust and smudges is to constantly polish them.

A young American who has practiced with me for over ten years frequently comes on retreats. After each retreat he takes the five precepts together with the other participants. He told me that at the end of a retreat he could take the precepts sincerely and uphold them purely at that moment. However, a month or so afterward he would begin to slip up. First he would break one precept, and he would say to himself, "Well, I broke one precept already, so what the heck?" After that it became easier to break the others. Then he would feel guilty and go on retreat again, where he would take the precepts once more. The interesting thing is that every time he takes the precepts, it takes longer before he breaks a precept again.

He asked me, "What do I do when I break the precepts?"

I told him, "You just need to repent."

He said, "But the precepts have been broken already."

I said, "Well, try to uphold them again."

This is what is meant by constantly protecting one's six senses— one needs to constantly uphold the precepts in order to keep the senses pure. It does not mean that taking the precepts will suddenly free you from ever erring again. The idea is that you try and when you fail, you repent and try again. When you are able to constantly protect your six senses, then you will realize the teachings in your internal and outward behaviors. And when you constantly protect your six senses, your behavior will be suitable for practice.

When you uphold the precepts, your actions and your speech will accord with the teachings, and as you cultivate the Seven Factors of Enlightenment, your mind will accord with the Dharma. Without protecting the senses it is very difficult to practice the Four Foundations of Mindfulness and the Seven Factors of

Enlightenment. One's mind will be confused and one's life in chaos. With a confused mind, you will be emotionally unstable, and with a chaotic life, you will have disharmony. Please make sure to protect your six senses when you embark on the practice of the Seven Factors of Enlightenment. Doing this is necessary to deal with the five hindrances.

OVERCOMING THE FIVE HINDRANCES

The purpose of the Seven Factors is to cultivate the wisdom based on contemplation, as well as the wisdom based on samadhi. Having gained the two kinds of wisdom, one uses them actively, but one has to keep the five hindrances—desire, anger, sloth, restlessness, and doubt—from arising, and if they arise, to cut them off. Then one needs to stabilize one's mind in order to cultivate the Seven Factors of Enlightenment.

To eliminate hindrances you must recognize them as soon as they arise. For example, greed may come from having favorable circumstances in one's life and craving for more. When one encounters unfavorable conditions one wants to reject them, giving rise to anger. If you are already tired when you start to practice, you may experience drowsiness. Excitement and stimulation will result in a scattered mind, making it difficult to stabilize the mind. Doubt comes from lack of confidence in the teachings, or lack of confidence in one's ability to practice. These five hindrances, so named because they obstruct our practice, are all obstacles to generating wisdom and compassion.

When you have a very good sitting, when your mind is calm and your heart is joyful, don't you wish it would last longer? Do you ever give rise to such thoughts? Or you may think, "Ah, this feels so good, I want to go deeper." Do you have thoughts like this? Yes, of course you do. This is one of the hindrances. Which one?

Students: Desire.

Sheng Yen: Yes, desire, in this case, greed for more. Therefore to practice the Seven Factors well, you will need not only learned friends but also the proper attitude.

A young professor was attending a retreat for the first time. During the first five days she suffered greatly. She kept saying to herself that the next day would be better, but every day her suffering actually increased. She told herself that if things did not get better by the fifth day, she was going to leave. She blamed herself for not having virtuous roots and not having the capacity to practice Chan. She decided that Chan was not for her and she stood up, getting ready to leave. At that moment she felt she had let me down, and that she had let down the Buddha. She felt embarrassed, so she bowed to the Buddha statue in the Chan Hall. In that moment all the physical discomforts that she had been experiencing vanished. She had been struggling and suffering so greatly for five days, and suddenly all those negative sensations were gone. She was so attached to her suffering that she could not let it go. The moment she gave up on that idea, her discomforts dropped away. She returned to her cushion and sat very well for the rest of the retreat. The difference was that she no longer wished her suffering to be gone, and she no longer rejected the discomforts of sitting. She was then able to practice very well, and at the end she did not want to leave. In fact, she plans to become a nun.

This is what it means to eliminate the five hindrances. Among the five hindrances, desire and anger are very difficult to overcome. So if you want to experience letting go of suffering, I welcome you all to our seven-day, fourteen-day, and forty-nine-day retreats. Or go on retreat forever by becoming a monastic practitioner.

SEQUENTIAL AND SIMULTANEOUS PRACTICE

Should one practice the Seven Factors sequentially or simultaneously? The answer to this depends largely on whether one practices in the Hinayana or Mahayana tradition, as well as on one's level of experience. In Hinayana Buddhism one practices the Four Foundations of Mindfulness to ultimately attain liberation. However in the Mahayana, one also practices the Four Foundations to help deliver sentient beings. We recognize that the early teachings are the foundation of later Mahayana Buddhism. Starting out with the Hinayana practices, it will be easier to gain power. To skip the foundation methods and jump right into the Mahayana methods is impractical, because we would be talking about methods that one's body and mind have not quite yet mastered. In fact, some people criticize Mahayana Buddhists for attempting to practice without first understanding the Hinayana foundations. They have a good point.

On a recent tour to China I visited several monasteries, one of them very old. I asked the people there, "Do you do practice Chan?"

They said, "Yes."

"What is your daily practice?" I asked.

They replied that they sat for ten periods a day, each period lasting as long as it takes for a stick of incense to burn down. Since a stick burns down in about an hour, that means they do sitting meditation all day.

So I said, "Many of you must be enlightened already!"

One of them said, "Not really, we are just training our legs."

I'm not saying that their practice is wrong. After all, in the Caodong (J., Soto) sect of Chan, the main practice is "just sitting" (J., shikantaza). Sitting that long every day for months on end is a real accomplishment, but the point is that practicing Chan is not just a matter of training the legs. One masters the Four Foundations of Mindfulness so one always knows what is happening in one's mind. Chan teaches that when we sit in meditation, we should always know where the body is and what it is doing, and that is true for the mind as well. You should be clearly aware of whatever thoughts arise in your mind, and whatever you are feeling. This actually is the cultivation of the Four Foundations of Mindfulness.

To practice the Seven Factors of Enlightenment, we begin by practicing each of them separately, after which we naturally practice them together. This is similar to the Four Foundations of Mindfulness, where we first practice each foundation separately and then we contemplate them together. At that point, when we contemplate one of the foundations we also contemplate the other three.

To use an analogy, in an extended family you have yourself, your spouse, your children, as well as the grandparents. When you think about taking care of your extended family, you think of them collectively. However when you actually help them, you address each person's particular needs. The problem is, when you take care of each person separately, inevitably you have preferences and possibly you discriminate between them. You may like some members of the family more than others, and so on. So taking care of the entire family at the same time reflects a higher level of ability.

Similarly, being able to practice all seven factors simultaneously reflects a deeper level of practice than practicing them separately. In the beginning one starts with one factor and proceeds step-by-step to the others. When you practice that one factor, you will know clearly what you are practicing. If you try to cultivate all seven factors at the beginning, you will end up not practicing any of them well. It is important to have the proper attitude for practicing the Seven Factors of Enlightenment.

DEALING WITH OBSTRUCTIONS

To cultivate the Seven Factors well, we need to eliminate obstructions, put down desires, and cut off vexations. These guidelines for daily life are difficult to live up to but as conditions for practice, they are essential. Removing obstructions means cutting off attachments to people, things, events, and anything in one's life that is an obstacle to practice. Putting down desires means departing from the five desires associated with the five senses, but also means not having ideas of attaining anything. Cutting off vexations means purifying oneself of the three poisons of greed, hatred, and ignorance, and knowing what to do when they arise. Before one is liberated it is impossible to have no vexations whatsoever. The important thing is that at least during the time that one is practicing, one tries not to give rise to any vexations.

One of my disciples had to choose between converting to another religion to marry his sweetheart or remaining single as a practicing Buddhist. I advised him that it was his decision to make. After agonizing over it he decided to marry the girl and convert. This story illustrates that in a dilemma, worldly desire can drastically alter one's spiritual direction. Getting married is not necessarily an obstacle to practice. Otherwise, one would have to become a monastic in order to practice. That is not the case at all. Anyone can practice the Seven Factors of Enlightenment. Shakyamuni Buddha taught the Noble Eightfold Path as well as the Seven Factors of Enlightenment. The Thirty-seven Aids to Enlightenment are taught to all practitioners, lay and monastic.

MINDFULNESS IS THE KEY

Although mindfulness is the first factor of enlightenment, in another sense it is also the last because it regulates the other six factors. Under what conditions do we practice the other six factors? In general, when one is lethargic, one practices the arousing factors: discernment, diligence, and joy. On the other hand, when one is unsettled, one practices the calming factors: lightness-and-ease, concentration, and equanimity. When you lack interest in the practice, you should focus on the arousing factors, and when you are unsettled, you should practice the calming factors. With the two complementing approaches, one is constantly cultivating both wisdom and samadhi. The common element among all the factors is mindfulness, which means being aware of our own mental states and practicing the right method for your situation. Without mindfulness it would be impossible to practice the other factors. One of the sutras says that when one is continuously mindful of the internal body, the external body, and the internal-and-external body, then one is cultivating mindfulness. At that time one will be able to cultivate the other factors.

This brings us back to the Four Foundations of Mindfulness and its practices of contemplating the realities of the body. We know that we have a heart, a liver, blood, tendons, and so forth, but we normally do not see or sense them except perhaps when we are ill. When we practice very well it is not that we can see our internal organs, but we are more aware of them. The external body consists of head, torso, trunk, and limbs, which we experience through our sense organs. The internal-and-external body refers to the integrated inner and external body. It can be likened to the case where one can take care of the entire extended family at the same time. Similarly, here you are contemplating both the internal body and the sense organs and the four limbs, all of the entire body simultaneously.

Don't be concerned that contemplating both the internal and external body at the same time would be too demanding. The main point is to realize that all the elements that make up the body do not make a self. The purpose of this contemplation is to really look into the question, "What is the 'self'?"

Contemplating the body is intimately related to contemplating sensations because sensations can only be experienced with the body. For example, when you sense that something smells nice or bad, do you sense it with your internal or external body? Probably both are true.

Sensations can be pleasant, unpleasant, and neither pleasant nor unpleasant. When we are mindful and aware of the quality of our sensations, we are contemplating sensations. We know whether they are pleasant, unpleasant, or neither pleasant nor unpleasant. Observing our reactions to sensations is contemplating the mind. The result of that mental reaction is a dharma, or mental object, and contemplating that is the fourth foundation of mindfulness. In our story about the young man asked to convert religions for the woman he loved, his desire for her became a dharma, a mental phenomenon. Or if someone gives rise to a vow to leave home and become a monastic, that idea also becomes a dharma in this person's mind. Starting from the contemplation of the body to the contemplation of one's sensations, and then one's mental reactions to sensations, and also to the dharmas arising from that, these four contemplations are the Four Foundations of Mindfulness. They are very critical for the cultivation of the Seven Factors of Enlightenment.

The philosopher Descartes said, "I think, therefore I am." His idea was that the ability to think was proof of the existence of the self. In Buddhism one looks at the self as made up of four elements, the first of which is the body. The second element of self is the sensations that the body experiences. The mental reactions to these sensations are the third element of the self. The dharmas, or ideas and concepts arising from one's mental reactions, make up the fourth element. If you can see clearly that what we call the "self" is really made up of these four elements, none of which have true selfhood, then you will be able to live with fewer vexations. If you are deluded or unclear about this, you will experience more vexations. That is why it is important to contemplate these four elements of body, sensations, mind, and dharmas.

Functions and Merits Gained from the Practice

The purpose of practicing the Seven Factors of Enlightenment is to cultivate samadhi and wisdom. As we develop the power of samadhi, we balance and stabilize our body and mind; as we develop wisdom, we reduce our suffering and vexations and enhance our ability to help others. Unless we clearly understand this, we may wonder whether the Seven Factors of Enlightenment have anything to do with practice. There are two aspects to using expedient means in practicing the Seven Factors. The first is to be always clear about your method, and the second is to regulate your body and mind according to the method. Following this approach, you will practice effectively.

What are expedient means? From the perspective of Buddha-dharma, any teaching transmitted through language, words, actions, or ideas is expedient means. A teacher with wisdom and compassion will instruct students according to their situation, understanding, and level of progress. This is expedient means. This is like a doctor prescribing the appropriate medicine for the patient's particular problem. There are all kinds of illnesses, all kinds of medicines, and all kinds of patients. Even a single patient may have different problems at different times. The doctor knows there is no one cure that will be effective for everyone at all times. Therefore the doctor prescribes for the patient's situation and needs at that time. Similarly, practitioners have different needs, and the teacher uses expedient means to help them.

Once I was out in cold weather without a coat. This lay gentle-man offered me his own coat. Wearing that coat, I did not look like a monk anymore. Another practitioner offered me her fur coat and said, "Shifu, my coat is warmer than that coat. You should wear mine." I did not think it was appropriate for me to wear a woman's coat, but she said, "Well, Shifu, what about expedient means?"

The Dharma itself is beyond words, but the Buddha needed to use words to help sentient beings depart from suffering. The words he spoke were dharmas of expedient means. So we have the Dharma, which is the ultimate truth of the Buddha, and we have dharmas, which are the language, words, and ideas used as expedient means to give the teachings. Even with expedient means, one should follow certain principles. Under some conditions, one may not be able to do much about someone's suffering. You may ask, "Although you look silly wearing a lady's fur coat, if you get sick you may not be able to teach. So isn't her offer expedient means?"

What do you think?

Student: What about the fact that the coat came from animals?

Sheng Yen: That is also an issue to ponder. Maybe you can use it as a koan. According to the precepts, a monk or nun may use a fur coat to keep warm, but the fur should come from animals that died naturally.

CONTEMPLATING EXTERNAL PHENOMENA

An example of expedient means is to use thoughts that arise in your mind to illuminate external phenomena. Remember though that external phenomena include things within your body that you can sense, whereas internal phenomena refer to thoughts arising in the mind. To cultivate samadhi you can collect your scattered mind by focusing on certain phenomena. One can concentrate one's mind either on a specific external phenomenon or on external phenomena as a whole.

Is the breath an external or internal phenomenon? A lot of people may think it's an internal phenomenon. When you think, "I am breathing," that thought is an internal phenomenon, but your actual breathing is an external phenomenon. So when you are observing the breath, you are already using the mind to focus on an external phenomenon.

There are people who meditate without a specific method, and very often, if they are not just resting or dozing, their mind is chaotic and fluctuating. In this scattered state they are basically watching a movie in which they are the scriptwriter, the director, as well as all the actors. They can be daydreaming about a girlfriend or boyfriend, or about making a lot of money, and on and on. When not practicing a specific method, watching a movie in your head is at least entertaining; otherwise one will get very irritated, feel very uncomfortable, and fidget a lot. In this kind of scattered state one needs an expedient means, such as a method for observing the breath. With this expedient means the chaotic thoughts can eventually be replaced by a single-minded focus on the method. It is very important to understand this principle of the method as expedient means.

TYING THE MIND TO PHENOMENA

Afte applying expedient means, the next step is tying the mind to phenomena and abiding in that. This means connecting one's mind to the phenomenon that one is focusing on. It is like this meditation bell here; as you can see, there's a little chain tying the bell to the striker so the striker does not get lost. Tying the mind to a phenomenon means that there is a linkage such that the object of focus does not get lost. This is like placing a banana in front of a monkey, but in a place where the monkey cannot reach it. If the monkey is hungry, he will sit and gaze at the banana for a long time. So while the monkey's mind is tied to the phenomenon, he is abiding in that phenomenon.

This is what Nagarjuna, the great Indian scholar, meant by tying the mind to a phenomenon—one is always focused on it, not forgetting that it's there. Abiding in the phenomenon means one's mind is so focused that it becomes very stable. If one's mind is not abiding in the phenomenon, it will be like the monkey wanting the banana but walking away every few moments, and then coming back. His mind is tied to the banana but is not abiding in it; he keeps losing his focus. That describes the state where one's mind is tied to the phenomenon but is not entirely stable yet. When one's mind is entirely stable, it will not lose its focus.

Once when I was using this monkey analogy, a student said, "I can totally relate to that, because this whole idea of tying the mind to phenomena is about cultivating samadhi, right?"

I said, "Yes."

And he said, "Well, that's what I did when I was pursuing this attractive woman."

I told him, "It's not the same thing. Instead of the clarity and calmness that one develops in samadhi, your mind was completely controlled by your desire." [*Laughter*]

When you can tie your mind to phenomena and abide in them, you can clearly perceive the previous thoughts as they fall and the subsequent thoughts as they rise. You know clearly the thoughts that just arose in the mind. You will be aware of the upward and downward movements of the mind. The upward movement of the mind is when one knows what's going on clearly, but there is also a feeling of excitement. The downward movement is when the mind is not as clear. In samadhi one's mind is supposed to be very stable, without upward and downward movements, but before entering samadhi it is almost impossible to have one's mind completely without any ups and downs.

The important thing is to make an effort to maintain a stable and even mind. If the mind gets too excited, it will become scattered; if the mind drifts downward too much, it will lose clarity. In the process of stabilizing the mind, it is normal to have upward and downward movement. When one is clearly aware of these movements, that is when one should perceive clearly the previous thought and the subsequent thought. Without the fluctuating movement, there will neither be previous nor subsequent thoughts. So the idea is to be very clearly aware of every thought, of every movement of one's mind, but at the same time not allowing the mind to move upward or downward too much.

A mind that is doubtful in the midst of practice is not sure what is going on or what one should do. "Should I do this or that?

Doing that felt nice before, but now it does not." And so on. This doubt is due to lack of confidence, an inability to gather mind-power in practice. At this point one needs to use the Seven Factors of Enlightenment properly in order to take care of the situation. For example, someone meditating may become drowsy. Then when they wake up, they will think that everything is fine, that they were meditating well. This sequence can recur again and again. There is nothing seriously wrong with this, but it is a downward movement of the mind where one becomes increasingly unclear, confused about what's going on, and doubtful.

The other case is when one has been sitting well and is excited about it: "I have been sitting well, and it's going to get better!" This is an upward movement of the mind, and you may find yourself having happy ideas, joyful thoughts. Then you may think, "I am sitting well, but can I keep it up, can I keep getting better? Should I be feeling good?" And this is doubt again.

So these upward and downward movements of the mind lead to doubt, and to constantly asking oneself questions. That is basically because one doesn't know whether one's situation is positive or negative. In principle it is a good thing to be sitting in a very calm and relaxed way. However, when one has been calm to the point where the mind has gotten dull, this means that the mind is unclear and moving in the direction of drowsiness. Also, in principle being relaxed is a good state. However, if one is so relaxed that the mind is getting too lax, then one is heading toward scattered mind. These are the situations that one needs to be clearly aware of, and know how to adjust accordingly.

Being aware of one's mental state is applicable not only on the cushion, but also in one's daily life. For example, there are people who are considered dull minded, who live in a kind of confused state, as if their brains were buckets of glue. There are also people whom we may call oversensitive, who react to things very quickly, actually sometimes overreacting. Some may think these people are a little crazy. These are polar states of mind that one can have in daily life, and they can even occur in the same person at different times. Perhaps I am one of those people. Sometimes when I don't quite know what's going on, Guoyuan Fashi [the abbot] tells me, "Shifu, you need to go do such and such." And I say, "Really?" But the same thing happens to him too, and I have to tell him. [*Laughter*]

Once we had a bodhisattva here who I asked to deliver an object to Guoyuan Fashi, and he said, "OK," as if he was going to do it right away. But in the meantime another person asked him to do something else in the basement. So he put my object down and went to the basement. While he was down there, somebody else wanted him to do something else. By this time he completely forgot about the thing that needed to be taken to Guoyuan Fashi. Originally I could have delivered this thing by myself. Now half a day had gone by, and this thing was still sitting in the reception area in front of the Guanyin statue.

When I saw that, I asked this person, "What happened? Didn't you take this to Guoyuan Fashi?"

And he responded, "What? You mean I didn't deliver it?"

So I ended up delivering that thing by myself, and this person said, "Shifu, I only have one pair of hands!"

I felt, "Well, he has a point." But although it is true he has only one pair of hands, he was still a little bit scatter-minded. Anyone can be scatter-minded once in a while, but one should recognize it and adjust one's mind so it stabilizes right away. If there are many things happening in daily life, one learns to take care of the things that need to be done one by one.

Practicing the Seven Factors of Enlightenment also helps one maintain the health of the body and the mind by calming the mind and eliminating vexations. This is because the practice requires both body and mind to be relaxed. This promotes mental health through keeping a stable and balanced mind, one that does not agitate easily and does not fluctuate all the time. Cultivating the Seven

Factors will help eliminate the vexations in one's mind so that our interactions with others are harmonious. Taking care of business, one will not be confused or doubtful.

A Review of the Seven Factors

The Seven Factors of Enlightenment are seven practices that guide us toward samadhi and wisdom. The first six factors—mindfulness, discernment, diligence, joy, lightness-and-ease, and concentration—focus on cultivating samadhi, while the seventh factor, equanimity, focuses on both samadhi and wisdom. The Seven Factors are important in the Hinayana as well as the Mahayana tradition, the main difference being that the Hinayana emphasizes samadhi, while the Mahayana emphasizes wisdom, including wisdom in daily life. Put another way, the Hinayana is more about individual practice; the Mahayana is more about relations in social settings. As one who received transmission in Chan Buddhism, I try to express the spirit of the Mahayana.

One Mahayana sutra, the *Vimalakirti-nirdesha,* has this passage: "Though [the bodhisattva] observes the Seven Factors of Enlightenment, [the bodhisattva] understands all the points of the Buddha's wisdom. Such is the practice of the bodhisattva."

This passage says that although one practices the Seven Factors of Enlightenment, one should not be limited by them. If one also realizes the Buddha's wisdom, then one is practicing the bodhisattva path. And what is the Buddha's wisdom? It is the wisdom of emptiness in which one's sees that all sentient beings possess buddha-nature. In the Hinayana there is no emphasis on seeing the buddha-nature in either oneself or others, while in the Mahayana, buddha-nature is seen as shared by all sentient beings. The fundamental difference between buddhas and sentient beings is that buddhas have seen their buddha-nature, while ordinary sentient beings have not. Therefore practitioners of the bodhisattva path should apply the Buddha's wisdom in daily practice and when interacting with people. This way, though one is not yet a buddha, one's behavior is in accordance with the Buddha's. When our wisdom is in accordance with that of the Buddha, our wisdom is the same as that of a buddha. The Hinayana goal is to obtain individual liberation. In this view, if other sentient beings have virtuous roots, they will eventually begin to practice toward liberation. On the other hand, in the Mahayana view, sentient beings are regarded as already being buddhas.

Some people may think that Westerners have a strong sense of individuality and are disposed to practice only the self-liberation path. That is not necessarily the case. Westerners, especially those that have a religious faith, believe that because God loves humanity, they should also love humanity. There is also among Westerners a very strong sense of justice, a belief that we should not tolerate unjust treatment of people. These sentiments in Western society gave rise to the ideas of democracy and equality. Were it not for such ideas, there would not be the American constitution, nor would slavery have been abolished. These principles are also in accordance with Mahayana Buddhism, which transcends culture and nationality. Now, let's consider how the Seven Factors are regarded in Nagarjuna's *Mahaprajnaparamita Shastra*.

MINDFULNESS

As we have said, in the Hinayana the first factor, mindfulness, is actually the cultivation of the Four Foundations of Mindfulness. The method begins by contemplating the body, and then contemplating the sensations experienced by the body. Since sensations are experienced by the mind, we next contemplate the mind's reactions to sensations. The mind's reactions to sensations are mental constructs, or dharmas. We then contemplate that dharmas are all just symbols or ideas, and after they arise, they disappear. We contemplate that these dharmas have the same nature as all phenomena, which are impermanent and empty.

What do you use to listen to this lecture? You use your ears. And where are your ears? In your head. And where is your head? On your body. That is contemplating the body. When you hear this talk, what do you hear? Whether you understand or not, at the very least you hear sound. What is sound? It is a sensation. That is contemplating sensations. How do you experience this sound? Do you find it interesting or boring? What is experiencing these sounds? Your mind is experiencing these sounds as interesting or boring. That is contemplating the mind. But these notions of "interesting" or "boring," what are they, and where do they come from? They are mental objects or dharmas; they are symbols, things that represent something else. This is contemplation of dharmas. This gives you a rough idea of how to practice mindfulness in the Hinayana tradition.

What is the Mahayana approach to mindfulness? The *Mahaprajnaparamita Shastra* says that the bodhisattva treats all experiences as phenomena—anything that the sense organs and the mind can experience, all sensations, feelings, objects, ideas, concepts, and events. This includes physical, biological, mental, emotional, and social phenomena. These can all be seen as phenomena. The shastra goes on to say that as bodhisattvas encounter phenomena, they immediately let go of them without any attachment. It is not that one does not remember anything, but that the memory does not become a burden. My memory is not that good, but I still remember a lot of things from my youth, the processes I went through, and the knowledge I acquired. Of course I have forgotten a lot. Even though I still remember many things, I never allow these memories to become a burden in my life.

In the Buddha's time, there was a scholar who knew everything there was to know about philosophy, religion, and other subjects. He wore a metal band around his head to keep it from bursting from all the knowledge inside. One time, he challenged the Buddha to a debate. This scholar said to the Buddha, "Ask me any question. If there is any question I cannot answer, I will become your disciple. Then I will ask you a question, and if you cannot answer, you become my disciple."

So Shakyamuni Buddha agreed to that. The first thing the Buddha said was, "Perhaps this is not quite a question, but it is about liberation."

The scholar said, "Well, ask me the question."

Shakyamuni Buddha kept silent while the scholar waited and waited for the question to be asked. Then he said to Shakyamuni Buddha, "Well, if you don't want to ask me a question, I will ask one. What is liberation?"

Shakyamuni Buddha still would not say anything. Finally the scholar became upset: "Why aren't you answering my question?"

Shakyamuni Buddha responded, "If one is already liberated, what need is there for questions?"

On hearing this, the scholar realized that his knowledge was useless, so he said to Shakyamuni Buddha, "I will be your disciple now."

This great scholar was so attached to all this knowledge he had which other people did not, and as a result he was not able to attain true enlightenment. In itself, having knowledge is not the problem. The problem is allowing knowledge to become a burden. If he hadn't been so prideful about his knowledge, this scholar would have had a better likelihood of being liberated.

DISCERNMENT

The second factor of enlightenment, discernment, is interpreted in the Hinayana tradition as knowing the difference between true and false Dharma, and following the true teachings and putting aside false teachings. The Mahayana approach can be seen in this passage from the *Mahaprajnaparamita Shastra:* "Seeking wholesome dharma, unwholesome dharma, or dharma that is neither wholesome nor unwholesome, these are all unattainable." For the most part, we respond to phenomena by seeing them as pleasant, unpleasant, or as neither pleasant nor unpleasant. However, when cultivating the factor of discerning between true and false, as described in the *Mahaprajnaparamita Shastra*, that should not be the case.

A student of mine who had been married about a month came to see me. I asked him how his new bride was doing. He said, "Before we got married, everything about her was good. After we got married, some things about her were good, some not good, and some things I really can't determine whether they're good or not." I thought that was interesting. Before he got married, everything was good, and afterward there's some good, some bad, and a new discovery of his wife. Is that the case with you, Paul, that after you got married you found your wife changing as well? [*Laughter*] Actually, I have heard the same thing from women. One woman, after getting married, told me: "Before my husband and I got married we went to a psychic to see if our horoscopes were compatible. The psychic said everything was fine. Before the wedding, my husband agreed to everything that I wanted, but afterward his real nature emerged; he began to grow a fox's tail." [*Laughter*] Do the Westerners among you know about [this Chinese saying] of someone growing a fox's tail? This means that someone you thought you knew turns out to be different after you have known them awhile.

I tell married people that they should adapt to each other's shortcomings because there is no such thing as a perfect person. They should try to understand and accommodate each other instead of being attached to the notion of an ideal spouse. There is no absolute good or absolute bad, and as one's attitude changes, one's environment will change as well. For example, some people think that if their spouse does something mean, their spouse does not love them. An outside observer might ask, "Why would anybody want to be with such a person?" But the mistreated spouse might feel that their partner really does love them, in spite of being mean occasionally. So there is nothing that's absolutely good or absolutely bad. It's all in one's perspective of what's going on. The thing is to understand that as one's attitude about what's going on changes, one's environment will change as well. This does not mean that there are no good people or no bad people, but that one should not allow other people's actions to give us vexation. When encountering these situations, you should handle them not with a mind of vexation, but with a mind of wisdom.

One scenario that sometimes happens is that a member of this center passes away and leaves behind a lot of Buddhist material—sutras, books, tapes, and so on. Sometimes the heirs are not Buddhist, so they will gather up these items and bring them to the center in boxes, leave them in the reception area, and say, "We have all this stuff for you." Then they leave without an explanation. So what do we do with all this stuff? Often we sort it out and leave it in the reception area for people to take. But we try to handle the situation without getting upset. There is no use getting upset, so we just take care of the matter.

DILIGENCE

In the Hinayana tradition, diligence means exerting oneself in practicing the Four Foundations of Mindfulness. In the *Mahaprajnaparamita Shastra,* Nagarjuna describes the Mahayana point of view. For him, diligence is exerting oneself to help sentient beings without being influenced by the three realms of desire, form, and formlessness. One should not be attached to the world of sentient beings; at the same time, one tries to deliver sentient beings from the three realms.

JOY

In the Hinayana, the fourth factor of enlightenment, joy, refers to the happiness that arises from the cultivation of dhyana. Speaking from the Mahayana view, the *Mahaprajnaparamita Shastra* says that when encountering phenomena, one does not attach to what is happening, nor does one give rise to vexation.

LIGHTNESS-AND-EASE

The fifth factor is lightness-and-ease. In the Hinayana, this is the dhyana of mental pliancy where one has no burden, either of body or mind. In this state there is no attachment to anything, no sense of wanting anything. This lightness-and-ease is equivalent to the first of the eight worldly samadhis. In the Mahayana view, one does not attach to the good feeling of lightness-and-ease; instead one sees it as an opportunity to practice simultaneous samadhi-and-wisdom.

CONCENTRATION

The sixth factor of enlightenment is concentration, or samadhi. This is the state where the mind remains on one thing without moving, where one knows clearly that there is no movement or chaos in phenomena at all. There is the same idea in the *Avatamsaka* (Flower Ornament) *Sutra,* which says that all dharmas (phenomena) are originally "thus," and have their own place in the world. In the Hinayana, samadhi is approached sequentially by beginning with the Five Methods of Stilling the Mind, and then proceeding to the Four Foundations of Mindfulness. In Chan practice, samadhi is attained simultaneously with wisdom, and can occur at any stage. This simultaneity of samadhi and wisdom can also be carried over into daily life. At that point Chan samadhi is also the samadhi of daily life. There is no gap between the two.

Equanimity

In the Hinayana, equanimity is the idea that as one continues in samadhi, one lets go of any mental state that one is experiencing. At a deep level of samadhi, any thoughts that occur are subtle and mostly symbolic, and even these must be let go. For the Mahayana, equanimity means that one does not attach to any phenomena, including a mind that lets go. There are neither phenomena that can be put down, nor a mind that does the putting down. This state is wisdom, or enlightenment.

6

THE NOBLE
EIGHTFOLD PATH

AFTER THE BUDDHA became enlightened, the first sermon he preached to his disciples was on the Four Noble Truths. The first noble truth, the Buddha said, is that suffering is a fact of existence; the second noble truth is that suffering results from our having wrong views; the third noble truth is that suffering can be ended; and the fourth noble truth is that the way to end suffering is to practice the Noble Eightfold Path, which consists of (1) Right View, (2) Right Intention, (3) Right Speech, (4) Right Action, (5) Right Livelihood, (6) Right Effort, (7) Right Mindfulness, and (8) Right Concentration.

If the way out of suffering is to practice the Noble Eightfold Path, how should we understand suffering? Actually, the Sanskrit word *duhkha* is conventionally translated as "suffering," but the term is nuanced and also connotes ideas of "unease," "disquietude," and "dissatisfaction." With that in mind, we can say that Buddhism recognizes three kinds of suffering. These are not three categories of suffering separate from each other, but rather three aspects of the experience of suffering as a whole.

The first kind is the suffering of suffering, the second is the suffering of change, and the third is pervasive suffering. The suffering of suffering consists of everything that we experience as part of being born, getting old, getting sick, and dying. In this sense to suffer is to experience samsara, the cycle of birth and death. This does not mean that in any given life there is no joy and happiness; sentient beings can know ordinary happiness and joy by satisfying the five senses. On another level, they can also experience the meditative bliss of samadhi. One who cultivates the Noble Eightfold Path can enjoy these kinds of happiness and still not attain liberation. Why? Because the happiness and joy derived from the senses and from samadhi are transitory. And because they cannot be maintained forever, the ultimate result is still suffering.

Suffering that results from the inherent impermanence of things is called the suffering of change. Underlying both the suffering of suffering and the suffering of change is pervasive suffering; it is a fundamental feature of sentient existence, so long as liberation has not been attained.

When someone praises you and you feel happy, is that true and lasting? On the other hand, if someone scolds you, is that also true and lasting? A treat of ice cream can be delicious, but if you ate one scoop after another, at some point would your pleasure turn to distaste? So the same experience may lead to joy as well as dissatisfaction.

Once in Taiwan a lay disciple brought me some loquats. I ate some of the fruit and told him it was delicious. The next time he brought ten pounds of the fruit and said, "Shifu, you seem to enjoy this fruit so much. Next time I will bring you more." If I tried to eat it all, would this be joy or suffering?

The Buddha did not deny that there is happiness in the world. However, the happiness and joy from sensual pleasure is brief and transitory. The bliss of samadhi during meditation can last for a while, but however deep the samadhi, one inevitably comes out of it; the samadhi will fade, and the joy will fade with it. Often one is left with a craving for more. This is an example of pervasive suffering—the subtle vexation that underlies the most blissful of feelings.

To experience true happiness, we need to cultivate the Noble Eightfold Path and attain freedom from vexations. The best kind of happiness comes when one is free from ever-conflicting thoughts and emotions. At that time, no matter what happens in the environment, favorable or not, one's body and mind will not be affected. One sees clearly that things are just the way they are. One no longer has a selfish need to benefit oneself. Both the burden of mind and the burden of body have been lifted. When the mind is without burdens, it is very clear and it responds to events appropriately and without vexation. When you are free of the burden of the body, then that is lasting samadhi. This is the joy of liberation.

When the Buddha's father died, Shakyamuni returned home to take care of the funeral. He also helped carry his father's body to the ritual ceremony. Do you think that at this time Shakyamuni Buddha's mind was filled with grief and suffering? If he had no grief in his heart, why did he go back to help with the funeral?

Student: Shakyamuni had sorrow, but without suffering.

Sheng Yen: Shakyamuni was a completely liberated being and therefore a buddha. But when his father died, Shakyamuni still needed to fulfill his responsibility as a son. Though Shakyamuni's father had heard the Dharma from his own son, he was not yet liberated. But Shakyamuni knew that his father would eventually become liberated. For these reasons there was no need for him to feel grief.

The Mahayana Path

In India at the Buddha's time, there was a belief that the purpose of life was to enjoy as much sensual pleasure as possible. Sensual pleasures are of course enjoyed through the sense faculties. This ability to experience pleasure through the senses gives rise to the five desires. In this hedonistic view, failing to fulfill the five desires results in unhappiness. In reality, however much we may crave and pursue pleasure, we can never completely satisfy the five desires. Therefore the result of constantly pursuing pleasure is vexation, not happiness and joy. Furthermore, this behavior ultimately causes conflict with others, producing more vexation. The sutras describe this kind of conduct as that of ordinary beings, not sages or saints.

Also prevalent in India at the time was the opposite view, that to become pure one needs to undergo extreme pain and suffering—the more pain, the purer one becomes. Some ascetics had themselves buried in the earth up to their necks; others would immerse themselves underwater for long periods of time, or hang upside down from a tree. Even today, in mainland China I saw one person who wore a very heavy coat in the summer but very little in the winter in order to inflict suffering on his body. In Taiwan I saw another person staring directly into the sun for hours. I asked him, "Why are you doing this?" He said that by staring at the sun he was burning off his bad karma. If such people think they can gain liberation through asceticism, then a furry dog running around on hot summer days can get liberated too.

Shakyamuni Buddha said that if following the path means suffering, the fruit will inevitably be more suffering. Inflicting suffering and pain on oneself will not result in liberation. Furthermore, the pains that ascetics inflict on themselves are not necessarily connected to the vexations they are trying to eliminate, and inflicting pain on one's body does not necessarily ease mental suffering. The Buddha therefore taught that the Noble Eightfold Path is the Middle Way between the opposing extremes of hedonism and asceticism. One needs the basic necessities of life in order to practice, but on the other hand one should not merely pursue pleasure for its own sake. So if one is guided by the Noble Eightfold Path, one will naturally practice the Middle Way. In other words, as long as the mind does not attach to this position or that, there is no discriminating self. But when one says, "I am neither on the right nor on the left, I am in the middle," there is still discrimination, and therefore there is still a self.

The ultimate goal of the Path is to realize no-self, which is the second meaning of the Middle Way. Whatever one experiences, thinks, says, or does, as long as a self is involved, one has not attained liberation. What then does realizing no-self mean? It means that one has no self-centered attachment to whatever one experiences.

Some Buddhists see practicing the Noble Eightfold Path as relevant only to the early Buddhism of the Nikaya scriptures. However, the later Mahayana scriptures do indeed advocate the Noble Eightfold Path. For example, the *Amitabha Sutra,* the *Vimalakirti-nirdesha Sutra,* the *Lankavatara Sutra,* as well as the *Mahaprajnaparamita Shastra* all advocate the Noble Eightfold Path as the foundation of the bodhisattva path. That is to say, the Noble Eightfold Path is correct Buddhadharma from the Mahayana point of view.

In early Nikaya Buddhism, the focus was on liberating oneself from suffering and entering nirvana, after which one need not return to the realm of sentient beings. Nevertheless, it would be a mistake to think that the liberation path and the bodhisattva path are separate. In fact, a proper understanding would be that they are two necessary stages of practice. Indeed, the *Saddharmapundarika* (Lotus) *Sutra* says that one who has just entered nirvana is like an intoxicated person who is not aware that there are sentient beings who are still suffering. However, these liberated beings eventually become aware that they should help sentient beings. At that time, they will give rise to bodhi-mind and engage in the work of delivering sentient beings by treading the bodhisattva path.

Once I met a man who told me, "Shifu, the Mahayana path is too much work. It involves helping and taking care of other people. I'm very selfish and I really don't have that much time. Could you teach me the liberation path so that I can free myself from suffering and vexations?"

I asked him, "Do you have a wife and children?"

He said, "Yes, I do, but that is precisely my point. My family is very annoying and irritating, and that's why I want to gain liberation."

I asked him, "If you became liberated, would you still keep your family?"

"Of course I would, but after I attain liberation they won't irritate me anymore."

That is quite idealistic thinking. I told him, "It's not that simple and you're not going to get away with it so easily. Even if you attain liberation and your family members have not, they will keep annoying you and attaching to you. You are still going to have vexations."

Just striving for liberation for oneself without being able to let go of everything in one's life is not truly attaining liberation. A better approach would be to help sentient beings give rise to fewer vexations. In that way one can be joyful and happy, and as a result one's family will not be a source of irritation. I told this gentleman that this is actually a very effective approach.

Another person often came to Chan retreats and was always very diligent in his practice. However because of his intense focus on practice, he neglected his wife and children. He even neglected his own career. As a result his family complained to me, "Shifu, our father has been studying the Dharma with you, but as a result we no longer feel secure. We feel hopeless. Is this the kind of result you're supposed to bring about in your teaching?"

So I asked this man, "Have you been studying Mahayana Buddhism?"

He said, "Of course, Shifu, you teach Mahayana Buddhism and that is what I practice. In fact, I practice very hard because I want to become liberated so I can deliver sentient beings."

I told him that, on the contrary, the bodhisattva path teaches that one vows to deliver others before delivering oneself. That is the correct way to arouse the bodhisattva mind, and that is how to practice the Mahayana path.

The Noble Eightfold Path is the essence of the Four Noble Truths in that it contains the methods through which sentient beings can be liberated from ignorance and suffering. In daily life people suffer from conflicts in their ideas, attitudes, and emotions. These kinds of suffering may seem similar, but they are different. Although conceptual conflicts can be resolved and clarified through logic and theory, psychological afflictions are not easily resolved through reasoning. In today's world there are many ideologies: some people praise the benefits of democracy, others argue for totalitarianism. There are also many faiths, each believing itself to be the best, and religious conflicts erupt into holy wars. All these types of conflicts are based on people having different worldviews.

Psychological problems, on the other hand, occur at a more personal level. People want to feel secure and gain as much benefit and happiness as possible. However, there are not so many opportunities. People are seldom content: they fear losing what they have, crave for more, and regret what they have lost. As a result, they never feel truly secure. These afflictions affect our sense of self, our health, and our relationships; we feel dissatisfied, unfulfilled, and unstable. These are all vexations.

A while ago we had guests from Taiwan, a mother and daughter. They planned to stay at the center for a week, but after just two days they disappeared without saying anything. We became so concerned that we called their family in Taiwan. The family informed us that the women were not there either. What is more, the family criticized us for not taking good care of our guests. Four days later the women showed up again.

I asked them, "Where have you been?"

They said, "We wanted to have some fun so we went to Las Vegas. It was so nice there that we decided to stay for a while."

I asked her why they did not tell us they were leaving, or call us. She responded, "Well, I'm not a member of the Chan Center, so why do I have to call you when I'm gone? We have to go now. Good-bye."

This is an example of vexation in social relationships. We cling to people and things; we can't detach from them. I did not have vexations before they showed up; after they showed up I had vexations.

The Noble Eightfold Path helps us resolve afflictions in the realm of concepts as well as emotions. The first two paths—Right View and Right Intention—help us deal with our erroneous views, and are perhaps the most important because they are the foundation for all the other paths. Right View is accomplished when one accepts the Four Noble Truths as the means for departing from suffering. When we view the world through the perspective of the Four Noble Truths, we are able to actualize them in thought, action, and speech. Applying the teachings of the Four Noble Truths, we can then depart from suffering and achieve happiness and joy.

Guided by Right View, we can investigate and truly understand what is around us. This will allow us to develop Right Intention and thus be able to manifest purity in our speech and actions. Purity means not causing vexation to oneself or others through words or actions. When our conduct is pure, this encompasses the next three paths: Right Speech, Right Action, and Right Livelihood. Then through Right Effort, we diligently practice meditation to achieve Right Mindfulness. With mindfulness as a foundation, we cultivate Right Concentration, or samadhi. When we cultivate deep samadhi, we can give rise to the wisdom that leads to liberation in nirvana.

Thus by following the Noble Eightfold Path, we can transform ourselves from suffering sentient beings into liberated saints with deep wisdom. The path is called noble because it facilitates our transformation toward sainthood and nirvana. Nirvana is the extinction of vexations, the cessation of the birth-and-death cycle.

In nirvana vexations no longer arise, and because they do not arise, they also do not perish. In the Noble Eightfold Path we practice the path of liberation while also aspiring to the bodhisattva path.

The Noble Eightfold Path can be seen from the point of view of the threefold division of Buddhist practice into precepts, samadhi, and wisdom. In this division, Right View and Right Intention comprise the paths of wisdom; Right Speech; Right Action, and Right Livelihood comprise the paths of precepts, and Right Effort, Right Mindfulness, and Right Concentration make up the paths of samadhi. I will discuss the eight paths in the order presented by the Buddha.

The Paths of Wisdom: Right View and Right Intention

RIGHT VIEW

Right View is the foundational teaching of the entire Noble Eightfold Path. Without Right View one cannot properly practice the Noble Eightfold Path. For a practitioner, not having Right View is like trying to drive on a mountain road at night without headlights. With Right View, traveling the Path is relatively easy—we understand that unless we cultivate the Path, we will surely experience continued suffering. Unless we understand that we create the causes of our own suffering, we cannot appreciate the importance of practice. However, it is also within our power to create the causes and conditions that can end our suffering. So both the aggregation of suffering and the cessation of suffering result from causes and conditions.

Soon after his enlightenment, the Buddha expounded the Four Noble Truths to his five original disciples. In this sermon he communicated just four ideas: suffering, aggregation, cessation, and the Path. Suffering is a fact of existence and is caused by our accumulating (aggregating) the causes of suffering. However, suffering can indeed be ended, and the way to cessation is through the Path. Therefore Right View is also precisely about the Four Noble Truths: understanding that this world is suffering, and knowing how we can depart from suffering.

As human beings living in this world, we need to acknowledge and understand that in life there is suffering. Where does this suffering come from? What causes it? Suffering comes from the countless past lives in which we have been creating karma. We create karma, and then we experience the retribution from that karma. At the same time, in this life we create more karma, and as a result we experience more retribution. That is what we have been doing life after life—creating karma and experiencing retribution. When karma is created we call that aggregation. And when causes and conditions ripen, retribution is experienced as suffering. Therefore we suffer because the causes of suffering still exist in our lives, and being ignorant of this we create more karma. In trying to escape suffering, we create more causes of suffering, and in pursuing happiness, we create more causes of unhappiness.

Therefore, to liberate ourselves from suffering we need to eliminate the causes of suffering. To stop a pot from boiling over, you remove the heat. If you want to stop suffering, you have to remove what causes suffering—the creation of new karma. To depart from suffering, stop creating more causes of suffering. Put simply, that is the approach.

We can speak of two kinds of cause and effect: first, worldly cause and effect that brings about the aggregation of suffering; second, world-transcending cause and effect that brings about cessation of suffering. Worldly cause and effect is that which creates more retribution karma, and world-transcending cause and effect is that which does not create retribution karma. Those who do not understand how suffering accumulates can be said to be ignorant, while those who do can be said to have wisdom.

Understanding the aggregation of suffering is the wisdom of

Right View, but it is not yet the wisdom of cessation and liberation, not yet the wisdom of nirvana. The Sanskrit word *nirvana* literally means "extinction," or in the Buddhist context, the state of non-arising and nonperishing. Having Right View is to understand that causes and conditions bring about the aggregation of suffering, and that causes and conditions also bring about the cessation of suffering. But this understanding is not enough for one to become liberated; one still needs to cultivate the Noble Eightfold Path.

Take a person who commits a crime and goes to jail. If he serves out his sentence, one day he will be free. Let's say that before his sentence is served, he tries to escape. He is caught and is sentenced to even more time in prison. Trying to put an end to his suffering by escaping, he creates more suffering for himself. Similarly, in order to be liberated from life's suffering, one needs to cease giving rise to the causes of suffering. It is not enough to want to stop unwholesome behavior and attitudes, because we have created a lot of karma in numerous past lives. This karma manifests as habit in our present life, and though we want to stop unwholesome deeds, we still have extremely strong entrenched habits. That is why it is necessary to cultivate the Path. We need the Path to help us regulate our actions, speech, and thoughts so that we will stop generating more causes of suffering and really bring suffering to a stop.

Unless we actually cultivate the Path, just understanding suffering and its causes will not help us that much. When we have problems we will still suffer, and we will continue to generate the causes for more suffering. Therefore it is important to also understand the meaning of samsara, which is made up of the cycles of our previous lives, our present life, and our future lives. A new cycle recurs every lifetime that we live without attaining liberation. These cycles of past, present, and future lives make up the transmigration of birth and death, otherwise known as the *nidanas*, or the Twelve Links of Conditioned Arising.

If we can understand how the links lead from one life to another, thus continuing the pattern of suffering, we will understand that to depart from suffering we need to cultivate the Path. That is how to generate wisdom and attain liberation. This transmigration will then cease because the first link in this chain, ignorance, or *avidya*, will have been dissolved. The Sanskrit term *avidya* translates in Chinese as "without brightness." In the ordinary mind, there is no brightness and no wisdom because they are obscured by vexations. If by cultivating the Path we eliminate vexations, then this ignorance will be eliminated as well, and wisdom will manifest. Once we eliminate ignorance, the remaining links will not arise. In this manner, the cessation of the cycle of birth and death is accomplished.

In Buddhism, there are three approaches or disciplines to cultivating the Path: upholding the precepts, cultivating samadhi, and generating wisdom. The first, upholding the precepts, has two aspects: regulating errors of the body and regulating errors of speech. Committing errors of the body means causing suffering to others with our actions; committing errors of speech means saying things that bring suffering to others. To cease causing further suffering through these kinds of mistakes, we need to constantly retake the precepts whenever we make such mistakes. This is what it means to uphold the precepts.

Merely upholding the precepts does not mean that one will no longer have vexations. It is also important to keep the mind stable and calm, so that no matter what happens in one's body or environment, one's mind does not suffer. Some uphold the precepts very diligently, yet still have internal conflicts and serious vexations. For example, they may have a strong desire for something, but they know that in order to uphold the precepts they should not give in to the desire. Still, if the desire is strong enough in their mind, they will be vexed. This is particularly true for romantic and sexual desires. A man will desire a certain woman but feel that he should not even be looking at her. Or a woman will hear gentle words from a man and feel that she should not allow herself to feel attraction. Such people may be very pure in their actions and would not do anything unwholesome, but these internal struggles are still vexations.

As long as there is desire, one is immersed in samsara, giving rise to more and more suffering. The reason why we can have vexations even though we uphold the precepts is because we do not have a mind that is stable and calm, one that is not affected by the environment. Therefore, besides upholding the precepts we should also cultivate samadhi to generate a calm and stable mind.

There are two approaches to cultivating samadhi: the gradual and the sudden. In the gradual approach one begins with the Five Methods of Stilling the Mind, then one proceeds to the Four Foundations of Mindfulness, progressing all the way through the rest of the Thirty-seven Aids to Enlightenment, ending with the Noble Eightfold Path. This gradual approach proceeds step-by-step toward becoming liberated as an arhat. In this process one will naturally cultivate samadhi as well as wisdom.

Instead of going step-by-step through the Thirty-seven Aids, the sudden approach of Chan proceeds directly to realization through such methods as huatou, or Silent Illumination. Through these practices one can cultivate a mind that is always in accordance with Chan samadhi. This is a direct way to attain a calm and stable mind, one that will not be affected by what's going on in the body or the environment. In the gradual approach, one first cultivates samadhi, and then the arising of wisdom follows; in the sudden approach, one cultivates and gives rise to samadhi and wisdom simultaneously. So is it clear now how one departs from suffering?

Student: Cultivate the path.

Sheng Yen: What path? One cultivates the Noble Eightfold Path. But what makes up the Noble Eightfold Path? The Path consists of the three disciplines of precepts, samadhi, and wisdom. Among the Noble Eightfold Path, Right View is the most important because it is the foundation for all the others. If one understands Right View, then the remaining paths will be relatively easy to understand.

Right View is a necessary aspect of wisdom, but it is not complete without also understanding the reality of phenomena. In my autobiography I wrote that I wept when I visited my parents' graves after being away for many years. A journalist who read this asked me, "Shifu, you are a highly attained monk. Why would you weep over your dead parents?"

I said, "I am not a highly attained monk, just an ordinary person. When my parents died, I couldn't even be by their side. When I returned, I could only find their gravestones. Knowing there was no way I could repay everything they did for me, all my feelings for them came to mind. It was impossible not to shed tears." Was I being ignorant, or is there some wisdom there?

Recently I did a pilgrimage to some of the sites where the Buddha taught. In one place I saw a memorial to the place where a great brahmin asked the Buddha to teach him Dharma. Upon seeing the monument, I knelt down and couldn't help but shed tears. One of my disciples asked me, "Shifu, why are you so sentimental, crying at the sight of this monument?" I said that I was crying out of gratitude to Shakyamuni Buddha for remaining in the world after his enlightenment in order to teach the Dharma. Had he not done that, we would not be able to hear the Dharma and use it to help ourselves as well as others. Therefore I am really moved and grateful to Shakyamuni. Is that ignorance or wisdom?

In 1977, when I had recently arrived in the United States, I received a call from Taiwan with news that my master Dongchu had passed away. I became very emotional and speechless. I just cried. A Dharma brother said to me, "Brother, you are not a child anymore. That your old master has died is a fact of life, so why are you crying?" The thought that I no longer had my master made me really sad. But then I felt grateful to this Dharma brother for reminding me that it is normal for old people to die. It was ignorant of me to feel so sad, but I couldn't help it because he was my master.

From the perspective of Right View, these stories have to do with the wisdom that comes from understanding the reality that all phenomena, including birth and death, have their place. Whatever roles we play in life—as parent, child, teacher, student—we should fulfill our responsibilities. We do not simply say, "Oh, dying is just proof of impermanence. If phenomena are empty and there is no self, why feel sad?" If one thinks this way, one is truly ignorant. From the perspective of Buddhadharma, we have our relationships, and we have responsibilities to fulfill. Denying their existence is an erroneous view. Before we are liberated we experience the causes and effects of the three times—past, present, and future—and denying that is also an erroneous view. On the other hand, affirming social ties as well as causes and effects is the Right View; it is the wisdom of understanding the reality of phenomena.

People fear death; they also fear the dangers in life, anticipating misfortune. Is that wisdom or ignorance? After returning to America from conducting a retreat in Moscow, I was very exhausted. One of the lay disciples took pity on me: "Oh, Shifu you are so exhausted, poor thing. With this SARS epidemic, are you sure you want to go to Taiwan?" Now, I am old and do not have a robust immune system, so this person was apparently worried. I told her there was a time when a lot of planes were crashing and people advised me not to travel by air. I told them that if it were time for me to die, it would happen whether I traveled by air or not. If it's not my time to die, that is because I still need to experience retribution karma. When it's time for me to die, it will happen. At the same time I am also very careful to take preventive measures. I am not going to Taiwan to get SARS on purpose, but I am nevertheless not afraid to go there. Is this ignorance or wisdom? If it is wisdom, it would be the wisdom of understanding the reality of phenomena.

Right View includes having the wisdom to accept the reality of phenomena. Just wanting to escape suffering would be failing in our responsibilities and denying causes and conditions. Wanting liberation without understanding the reality of phenomena is an erroneous view. Therefore I offer you these words to remember: "Before liberation one ought to fulfill one's responsibilities; before attaining buddhahood one should first be a good person." This is the wisdom of understanding the reality of phenomena.

Attaining the wisdom of nirvana is our ultimate goal, but the wisdom of understanding the reality of phenomena is the process. The wisdom of nirvana is realized when one has attained self-understanding, self-verification, and self-enlightenment. When that happens, one has accomplished everything that one needs to on the Path. It is the complete realization of understanding the reality of phenomena. At this time there is no longer any arising and perishing of causes and conditions. This is the wisdom of nirvana.

Verification means that we completely understand that life arises from causes and conditions, and also perishes with causes and conditions. We recognize two kinds of arising and perishing. One is the arising and perishing of the entire life of the body that we now have. This begins with conception in our mother's womb and ends with death. Second, within one's life there is also the moment-to-moment arising and perishing of microscopic events in the tissues and cells of our body. This is the process by which we grow, mature, get old, and deteriorate both in mind and in body. This is all due to the moment-to-moment arising and perishing that goes on within the larger arising and perishing of birth-to-death.

Two years ago I met an elderly practitioner who could recite the entire Surangama Mantra, which is very long. I said to her, "It's very good that you can recite the entire mantra even though you are an older person." She said. "Oh, this mantra is nothing; I can recite the entire *Surangama Sutra*." She has known the mantra since she was young, so she knew it by heart. A year ago I met her again and learned that she was no longer reciting the Surangama Mantra, but another shorter mantra. I asked her why she was not reciting the Surangama Mantra anymore. She said, "Oh, the Surangama Mantra is way too long and wordy. I'm reciting a mantra that is more concise." But the truth was that she could no longer remember the whole mantra. This past spring I saw her again and this time she was reciting an even shorter mantra, the Mantra of the Deceased. I am afraid that next time I see her she will be reciting only Amitabha Buddha's name. Within the larger arising and perishing of one's life, there are many smaller arisings and perishings, and memories are among them.

Therefore the idea of arising and perishing refers not only to our entire life; more importantly, it also refers to every moment of our life. With the wisdom of nirvana we understand very clearly that in every mental, physical, and environmental phenomenon, there is simultaneous arising and perishing. As soon as dharmas arise, they are already perishing. Each of you here, do you believe that in every moment there is constant arising and perishing in your body? In fact, if this were not the case, you would not even be alive. For living things, there must be motion and change. If there is no change, there is no life. As long as we are alive there is metabolism: cells and tissues constantly moving and transforming. How about when we're dead? Actually, when we die we change even faster. Therefore those who have realized nirvana, those who have attained self-verification, clearly understand that everything that arises simultaneously perishes. Whatever arises is on its way to perishing. But from where do things arise? Things arise out of causes and conditions.

This is different from the view that we are all creatures of a God, and when we die we return to that Creator. The Buddhist view is that everything arises and perishes due to causes and conditions. The Buddhist scriptures do not deny the existence of a God who created everything; rather, out of myriad causes and conditions a deity would have been born along with the universe. In Hinduism, this is the Brahman God-King who lives until the death of the universe. When the universe disappears, the Brahman God-King disappears with it. This Brahman God-King does not experience human mortality, and therefore appears eternal. From the perspective of a buddha, this world is only one of myriad worlds, all of which arise and eventually perish. Buddhists do not say that belief in God is superstitious. However from the Buddhist perspective, even such a God must experience birth and death. Therefore in the wisdom of nirvana, there is a very clear understanding that all phenomena, even universes, experience arising and perishing.

So if one looks at the stage between the birth of the universe and its death, there is arising and perishing, and within this period there are also infinite momentary arisings and perishings. Take planet Earth, which is undergoing constant moment-to-moment arising and perishing. These changes occur on other planets as well. One can only completely attain this wisdom after one has realized nirvana, which it why it is called the wisdom of nirvana.

To the question, "From where does everything arise?" the wisdom of nirvana answers that things do not arise from anywhere. Rather, everything arises from causes and conditions. We think, "Oh, I'm from Taiwan," or "I'm from India," as if there is something from these places that could come to America. There is something that comes from those places, but from the perspective of the wisdom of nirvana, that something arose from the coming together of causes and conditions in every moment. So I was born as a result of many causes and conditions coming together, including karma that I created from previous lifetimes. Then there were my parents, the environment I grew up in, whatever I consumed growing up— that's how I arose. According to physiology, our body replaces all its cells every seven years, so if I stayed here for seven years and only ate Western food, after seven years I would have a Western body even though I would still look Chinese. You see the point: our body is undergoing arising and perishing all the time.

Several years ago a mother brought her teenage boy here. When I asked him, "Are you Chinese or American?" this boy said, "I'm American." And I asked, "How about your mother?" "Oh, she's Chinese." Upon hearing that the mother was very upset: "This kid can't even remember his own heritage!" I said to her, "Well, he is right. He grew up here in America, he eats American food; everything he has experienced is American. Of course he is American. And you came from China and grew up in Taiwan, your experiences all came from Chinese society. Of course you're Chinese." Upon hearing this, the child was very happy: "I'm right, I'm American."

According to Dharma, all phenomena arise from a nexus of causes and conditions that are in constant flux. Therefore as phenomena arise they are still subject to causes and conditions, and are therefore subject to change. And because phenomena change, they ultimately perish. And to where do they perish? They don't perish to anywhere; they become new causes and conditions for further arising and perishing. From the perspective of the wisdom of nirvana, there is no place to which phenomena perish. Nirvana means extinction; it means no arising and therefore no more perishing.

RIGHT INTENTION

The second noble path, Right Intention, is also referred to as Right Thought, Right Discernment, or Right Enlightenment. The essence of Right Intention is to use the Right View that one has acquired. One could say that when we have Right View, Right Intention should follow. This does not mean just thinking about it abstractly, but to understand it through the practice of meditation, or dhyana. With the resulting clarity and stability of mind, we will be able to understand phenomena from the perspective of the Four Noble Truths. For example, normally we are pleased with our body, but at times the body is also a burden and a source of suffering. The body is not entirely under our control—we get sick, we age, we die. And if we try to relieve or suppress the problems of the body, this may result in more suffering. Observing the body and the mind with Right Intention, we come to understand that impermanence is at the root of suffering. This is an opportunity for some wisdom to arise, but an intellectual understanding of suffering is not enough to liberate us from suffering. One needs to perceive as well that suffering is also illusory and empty, and so is the self that suffers. Only when we thoroughly penetrate this understanding of emptiness and no-self can we depart from suffering.

I met someone who felt that his life was filled with so much suffering that he did not see much point in living. He saw his body as falling apart, capable of dying anytime. From his point of view, one may just as well commit suicide to escape suffering. Is there wisdom in thinking this way? Actually, while having some understanding of impermanence, he does not understand that there is also emptiness and no-self. Theoretically, understanding impermanence should lead one to understand emptiness as well as no-self, but that is only conceptual. Without experiential realization of emptiness, this person is unable to see that there is no self behind the suffering. He does not understand that wanting to end one's life is actually clinging to the self because it is the self that wants to escape.

There can be no true realization of emptiness when we cling to the self. To truly realize emptiness, one needs also to give rise to bodhi-mind. In fact, emptiness and bodhi-mind are two sides of the same coin; one cannot truly realize one without the other. Trying to realize emptiness without giving rise to bodhi-mind can only result in a nihilistic kind of emptiness. That will not help one depart from suffering, nor experience liberation.

The mind of bodhi is not centered on one's own problems, so when we are suffering, at that moment we should be more concerned about the suffering of others. When I am ill, I use Right Intention and think about the infinite number of beings who are suffering more greatly than I am. This way I hope to use the power of my vows to help deliver people from suffering. In that moment, of course I haven't really decreased anybody's suffering, but just by giving rise to that thought I am already suffering less. So giving rise to bodhi-mind and thinking about the suffering of others can definitely help to decrease one's suffering. For example, if you feel that you lack certain necessities, remind yourself that many people have even less. In your bodhi-mind, give rise to the wish that they will all have a better situation soon, and that you will form an intention to help those who have less than you. You will find that this thought will bring warmth to your mind, and you will feel less unfortunate.

On one seven-day retreat, a participant was in so much physical pain that she felt like she was in hell. Feeling that practice was not for her, she was about to leave the retreat. I said to her, "Perhaps you can go back to the Chan Hall to deliver other sentient beings."

"How am I supposed to deliver sentient beings?" she asked.

I told her, "When you go back to the Chan Hall, tell yourself that you are there to sit well and inspire your neighbors to practice diligently."

She accepted my suggestion and went back to the Chan Hall. There she thought, "My body aches, but if I am not willing to go to hell to help others, who will?" By thinking this way, she had a very good retreat.

After studying Buddhadharma and the teachings of suffering, impermanence, and no-self, someone can conclude that they have experienced emptiness. While thinking that, this person may continue to suffer a great deal. This person understands that everything is empty and without self, but their suffering is there and it's real. So with all this understanding of emptiness and no-self, there's still a lot of suffering. What is missing here is bodhi-mind. When you have bodhi-mind, you will not be so concerned about yourself. When you put the welfare of other sentient beings at a higher priority than your own, you will naturally be less concerned about yourself. When you are not so attached to your ego, you are already experiencing no-self and realizing the nature of emptiness.

Emptiness does not mean that there is nothing there; it is the idea that you are not so attached to your self-concerns. When you are less attached to yourself, you can begin to have a true understanding of emptiness, and then you are able to give rise to wisdom. When you can do that, you are on the path toward liberation. You will be able to depart from the five worldly desires of wealth, sex, fame, food, and sleep, and truly be able to depart from suffering.

The Paths of Precepts: Right Speech, Right Action, Right Livelihood

If Right View and Right Intention are the paths that comprise wisdom; Right Speech, Right Action, and Right Livelihood define ethical behavior, or precepts.

RIGHT SPEECH

The third noble path is Right Speech, also called True Speech, or Noble Speech. Right Speech means speaking only what is true. The *Diamond Sutra* says that a buddha does not engage in the four kinds of unwholesome speech: lying, vulgarity, slander, and frivolous talk. Lying means saying what is untrue, vulgarity means using improper language, slander means defaming other people and causing disunity, and frivolous speech means saying meaningless things, including idle chatter.

The true purpose of speech is to enable us to express ideas, opinions, and feelings in social interactions, and to bring comfort, benefit, encouragement, and happiness to others. When we use speech for these purposes, we benefit ourselves as well. Speech that causes harm to other people is not Right Speech, regardless of the manner in which it is said. One should not hurt others with words and then say, "I said it in a nice way; I didn't mean to cause harm." But if what you said caused harm, that is not Right Speech.

Speech is also properly used to express wisdom and, most important, compassion; its purpose is not for venting our own emotions and frustrations, nor to fight, conquer, or suppress other people. There are people who rarely speak, but when they open their mouth they scold and criticize. As long as your speech discomforts other people, that is not the practice of Right Speech. A Buddhist teacher might say to their students, "I have been teaching you Buddhadharma and you should show more compassion." Or "You people have no wisdom at all." Speaking this way is not in accordance with Right Speech, and such a teacher has neither compassion nor wisdom.

A young couple who had been married for two years fought all the time. The wife would complain to the husband and say, "You are the only person in my life. I always think about taking care of you in the best way and making your life comfortable. I'm willing to sacrifice everything just for you, so why are you so cold to me?"

The husband responded, "Before I got married, I ate, slept, and put on my clothes in the same way I do now. I don't need you to take care of me."

They speak to each other in this vein all the time. So this wife felt very frustrated and upset and came to me for advice. I suggested that she tell her husband that she takes such good care of him because she needs his help in return. She went back and tried this, and it was very useful. It gave the husband a sense of accomplishment, a feeling that he was being helpful to her.

How you use words can make a difference. If you express an idea in a way that makes the other person comfortable and happy, you also benefit from the interaction. If you express the same idea in a way that makes the other person uncomfortable, you also suffer the consequence. Therefore when you go back and interact with your family and friends, if what you say makes them feel happy, you are practicing Right Speech. If what you say makes them feel unhappy or uncomfortable, or makes them suffer, at that moment remind yourself, "I'm not practicing Right Speech."

When longtime practitioners seem to suffer a lot, some people may ask, "Why do some Buddhists who practice so much still suffer a great deal?" In part that may have to do with their not paying attention to Right Speech, not making sure to express themselves in ways that bring happiness and harmony in their relationships. It is truly important to express yourself in ways that bring happiness and harmony to others. That way you will truly be able to depart from suffering. When people treat you unfairly or unjustly, you may feel an urge to respond by hurting them through speech. Instead, you should give rise to compassion and bodhi-mind, and hope that the other person will behave more harmoniously in the future. That way you will not automatically be so upset or feel the urge to react with unwholesome speech. If you allow yourself to get upset, you are no different from the other person. By practicing Right Intention, you will be able to handle the situation and avoid giving rise to more ignorance.

RIGHT ACTION

Right Action, or Noble Action, is the idea that our every action should accord with Buddhadharma. Right Action also refers to the elimination of the three kinds of unwholesome bodily conduct: killing, stealing, and sexual misconduct. For laypeople, sexual misconduct means sex with anyone other than one's spouse. For monastics, sexual misconduct means any kind of sexual interaction. The reasons why people commit the three kinds of unwholesome acts are not having the Right View, giving in to greed or desire, and harboring hatred or aversion. Not having the Right View, people will not be able to see this kind of conduct as improper. Other erroneous views are thinking this sort of unwholesome conduct will yield certain benefits such as fame, power, wealth, or health. Greed and desire can bring about unwholesome conduct when we have desires that we think we need to satisfy. And because of hatred and anger, people want to hurt or retaliate against others, to vent their emotions and frustrations by killing, stealing, or sexual misconduct.

What causes the conflict between nations and cultures that makes them kill each other, such as we have today? Part of the answer is hatred and the perceived need for retaliation. It is also because of ignorance about the unwholesome consequences of war and conflict. The same logic applies to stealing and sexual misconduct. Some people steal out of hatred or a wish for vengeance. This can take the form of stealing property, someone's spouse, or in fact an entire nation. The same thing applies to sexual misconduct, which can also be caused by hatred as well as desire. But if one can give rise to compassion and bodhi-mind, one will not give rise to these kinds of unwholesome conduct.

From the positive side, Right Action expresses love for sentient beings and the desire to be very protective of the environment in one's own life, as well as at large. It also means engaging in a healthy and harmonious sexual relationship with one's spouse only, as well as not thinking only about oneself and not harming individuals or the community. Furthermore, one should cultivate positive relationships with people, engaging in charity and so on, while at the same time giving oneself happiness. Positive relationships and charitable acts are therefore two proper paths to Right Action. As far as charity is concerned, one should not indiscriminately give to every cause or to everyone who asks, but give to the right people, at the right time, in an appropriate way.

RIGHT LIVELIHOOD

Right Livelihood is the true way to secure the necessities of life, and the proper way to conduct oneself in daily life. The conventional sense of livelihood is earning a living, but Right Livelihood means doing that in accordance with wisdom and compassion. This means not causing vexations and afflictions for oneself or others. It is not

Right Livelihood if your job causes others to lose theirs; securing one's livelihood should not cause unhappiness to others. A livelihood that brings a lot of security and safety but makes other people insecure and unsafe is also not Right Livelihood, and not compassionate.

When taking a job, people should consider whether it is legal or likely to bring a lot of vexation. There are livelihoods that are legal but may cause harm to others. Knowingly taking such a job is not wisdom or compassion. For a lay practitioner, the main principle is to make a living while upholding the five precepts. What occupations would involve violating the five precepts? Foremost would be a job that requires killing sentient beings, especially humans. The second precept forbids stealing, so this would exclude jobs that involve getting other people's property improperly. Clearly, one should not take a job that entails sexual misconduct, which is forbidden by the third precept. Fourth is the precept against lying, so occupations that involve deception and saying untruthful things are to be avoided. The fifth precept, no use of intoxicants, precludes making a living dealing in illegal drugs or addictive gambling.

To summarize, occupations that contradict upholding the precepts, that cause harm to people and chaos to society, should not be taken by practitioners. At first glance some of these occupations seem to bring much benefit to oneself, but if one looks at them more clearly there can be more harm than benefit. For example, people who are involved in slaughtering animals may think they are just offering a service to society. However, killing animals causes suffering to them and is not a very compassionate way to make a living.

Someone who took refuge with me comes from a family who have been pig farmers for three generations. Their farm has about a thousand pigs at any given time. The pigs are ready for slaughter at three or four months, and in a typical year this farm processes about three thousand pigs. This disciple told me, "Shifu, I'm very compassionate in taking care of my pigs. I make sure that they are fed well, I get them pretty chubby; I love these pigs."

I asked him, "What happens to these pigs after you take care of them?"

He said, "We sell them to the slaughterhouse."

"What happens in the slaughterhouse?"

"Well, they get slaughtered." Then he said, "Yes, those people who work in the slaughterhouse, they could use some help to reform their mind."

I asked this person, "Could you bring these people to me so that I can give them help and reform them a little bit?"

So this disciple brought the two owners of the slaughterhouse to me. I asked them, "Of all the possible occupations, why slaughtering pigs?"

One of them said, "Shifu, actually I am really very compassionate. In the past, pigs were slaughtered in a really cruel way. We worked very hard to figure out a system to kill pigs in a humane way, so these pigs are very fortunate. Besides, it's all because people want to eat pork."

I said to them, "Nevertheless, these pigs are still being slaughtered."

One of the owners said, "Master, even if we do not kill these pigs, other people would be doing it. So if you truly want to deal with this problem, get people to stop eating pork. It is the people who eat pork who are not compassionate."

Two other people witnessed this conversation. I asked them, "Do you agree that if people stopped eating pork, there would be no need for people who slaughter pigs? Do you eat pork?"

Their response was, "Well, it's not that we have to eat meat, it's just that everywhere we go they serve meat. If they stopped slaughtering pigs there would be no meat in the restaurant, and we wouldn't eat it anymore. It's out of our control."

As you can see, this is a very interesting cycle. The slaughter-house people say it's because of the demand for pork, the meat eaters say it's because meat is served to them. Neither admits responsibility and they all claim to be compassionate. What do you think?

Student: This sounds very familiar because most people are meat eaters. When we abstain from meat, our families criticize us and our co-workers make remarks, so it is a familiar problem.

Sheng Yen: You happen to be vegetarian. Maybe other people would disagree with you.

Student: Other people think that I'm not very compassionate toward carrots and broccoli!

Sheng Yen: One can distinguish between living things that have a nervous system and memory versus those that don't. Human beings and higher forms of animals that have a nervous system and memory are capable of suffering. Some simple forms of life have a nervous system, but they don't have memory. Plants have cells, but no nervous systems and no memory. Buddhism considers it uncompassionate to eat living things that have a nervous system and a memory because they are capable of suffering. Plants lack a nervous system and are not unlike fingernails or hair, which are nourished by our circulatory system but do not experience pain when cut. Out of compassion one refrains from killing or eating animals because we don't want to cause them fear and suffering. Therefore for Right Livelihood we should avoid any occupation that involves killing animals. Refraining from causing harm to others is not just directed to animals; in fact the emphasis should be on directing compassion to other human beings.

The second precept prohibits stealing—taking something from others without their permission—or robbery, taking something by force. Quite a number of occupations in the world involve stealing or robbing. Piracy is a vivid example of a profession that involves robbing people by force.

There was a case in Taiwan about people who went to a remote

THE NOBLE EIGHTFOLD PATH

national park to collect rock specimens and rare medicinal herbs, which they would then sell. Somebody discovered what they were doing and reported them to the authorities. At a trial, the defendants claimed that the rocks and herbs were just lying there, and nobody was using them anyway. They claimed that they were performing a service that created wealth for society, but the court found them guilty. These people had the wrong livelihood.

Right Livelihood means securing one's livelihood while following the Buddhist principles of wisdom and compassion. Laypeople have families as well as careers, so upholding the precepts is adequate to ensure that one is practicing Right Livelihood. Those who have left home (monks and nuns) are supported by the offerings of followers and disciples. There is no need for them to engage in jobs or careers to secure their daily necessities. In fact, monastics are not allowed to earn money for material necessities. However, the standard for Right Livelihood in Buddhist monasteries can also vary across cultures. For example, in India during Buddha's time, monks were supported by the laypeople and by the royalty, so that their material needs were provided for. Also, Indian monks went around with an alms bowl, receiving offerings from the public. In China, laypeople also provided support for the monastic community, but not to the same level as in India. For Chinese monks and nuns, farming was part of Right Livelihood and there was no strong mendicant tradition.

In olden times, it was considered improper to sell Buddhist sutras, which were supposed to be given away free as a way to help sentient beings. To sell a sutra would be like selling the Buddhadharma and was not considered Right Livelihood. When I was a young monk in China, if a Buddhist master charged a fee for teaching Dharma, he would be described as making money off the Buddhadharma. The problem in contemporary society is that if there were no admission fee, it would be difficult to raise enough money to maintain or rent facilities for teaching and practicing. I once asked a famous

Buddhist teacher if charging admission for a lecture was selling the Buddhadharma. He replied, "The proper way for them to think of it is that they are making an offering to the Buddhadharma."

The Paths of Meditation: Right Effort, Right Mindfulness, Right Concentration

The complete Buddhist path consists of the three disciplines of precepts (morality), samadhi (meditation), and wisdom (bodhi or awakened mind). When one practices the Noble Eightfold Path, one also practices the three disciplines: Right View and Right Intention make up the study of wisdom; Right Speech, Right Action, and Right Livelihood make up the study of morality; and Right Effort, Right Mindfulness, and Right Concentration make up the study of samadhi, or meditative concentration.

RIGHT EFFORT

Right Effort is also called Right Diligence, or Right Discipline, or the Noble or True Dharma. This is the path of practicing Buddhadharma with continuous dedication. Specifically, we mean diligent cultivation of the Four Foundations of Mindfulness. The purpose is to gain the path of liberation and give rise to wisdom. As we practice the Four Foundations, we also rely on the Four Proper Exertions to maintain diligence and eliminate vexations. In fact, the only way to practice the Noble Eightfold Path ceaselessly and without regressing is through the Four Proper Exertions. This is called Right Effort, and the best way to practice it is by establishing a foundation of practice in the first five noble paths, namely, Right View, Right Intention, Right Speech, Right Action, and Right Livelihood.

Even though Right Effort is the sixth path, it encompasses all the others. This is because diligence is necessary to successfully cultivate any of the paths. So it is not the case that in Right Effort there is just this focus on diligence in and of itself. Rather, it is the equal emphasis on all three studies of precepts, concentration, and wisdom. So Right Effort means that you should avoid any hindrances to upholding the precepts. Similarly, one avoids all the obstacles to cultivating deep concentration. One needs to depart from all the hindrances to attaining wisdom, in whatever form or shape. This is how to practice Right Effort. However, just avoiding obstacles is a negative approach; one should also uphold the precepts, practice concentration, and cultivate wisdom. You may think, "I have to avoid all the obstacles and at the same time diligently cultivate the three disciplines! Can I do that?"

My answer is not to worry—every one of you can do it.

RIGHT MINDFULNESS

Although the Noble Eightfold Path is just one part of the Thirty-seven Aids to Enlightenment, the proper understanding is that it actually encompasses the whole of the Thirty-seven Aids. In fact, cultivating any of the seven groups in the Thirty-seven Aids can help one depart from vexation and attain liberation. The difference is that the Noble Eightfold Path is the most complete path of all. Remember that the basic teaching of the Buddha is the Four Noble Truths, and the fourth noble truth is that the way out of suffering is through the Noble Eightfold Path. In turn, the first noble path is Right View, which one has when one understands the Four Noble Truths. In other words, the Noble Eightfold Path includes all the concepts as well as methods for living ethically and morally, cultivating samadhi, and attaining wisdom.

The seventh noble path is Right Mindfulness, and it refers to the Four Foundations of Mindfulness: mindfulness of the body, mindfulness of sensations, mindfulness of the mind, and mindfulness of dharmas (phenomena). Buddhadharma teaches that suffering is caused by our holding wrong views about these four categories. Therefore the purpose of contemplating them is to be liberated from vexation. Seeing our body as pure is a wrong view because the body deteriorates, gets sick, and dies; viewing sensations as pleasurable is also erroneous because sensations also cause suffering; seeing the mind as the self is erroneous because it leads to egocentric attachment; and finally, viewing dharmas—the body, the mind, and the environment—as either belonging to or opposed to us also causes vexation. Because we hold these erroneous views, we constantly experience vexation and suffering.

Because the Four Foundations are so fundamental to cultivating the path, I would like to briefly review them here.

Mindfulness of the Body

To overcome our wrong views, we should first contemplate the true nature of our body. When we are young our body is healthy, soft, and sweet smelling, and it is easy to love it. However, as we age we are often not at ease with this body and can't seem to gain control of it; it does not smell so nice and we realize it is not so pure anymore. I ask you, are you mostly satisfied with your body? Is it different now than before?

Once on a retreat I was teaching everyone how to clean up after a meal. I asked them to pour hot water in their bowl, rinse their utensils in the water, and finish by drinking the rinse water. When one participant refused to do it, I asked him, "Weren't you just now eating from this bowl?"

He said, "Yes."

And I said, "Well, you were using the chopsticks, and it's your mouth that's been touching them. So what is wrong with drinking the water?"

He said, "But that's disgusting! It's like drinking dishwater."

I asked him if he ever kissed his girlfriend.

"Yes," he said, "of course."

I asked him, "So is your girlfriend clean?"

He replied, "Of course my girlfriend is clean!"

I said, "But if your girlfriend ate something and spat it out, would you go ahead and eat it?"

He did not answer. He is willing to kiss his girlfriend, but not willing to eat something that came out of her mouth. This comes from an erroneous view as to what is pure and what is impure. If something is clean, isn't it clean in all situations? If it's dirty, isn't it dirty in all circumstances? Where does the discrimination come from? So when we practice mindfulness of the body, we are reminding ourselves that ultimately the body is not always pure, and we should not become too attached to it. Yes, we should take good care of the body and protect it. However, we should refrain from attaching to the idea that this body is always so great and wonderful. The body is sometimes pure, at other times not so pure. As we age, we experience the impurity of the body more and more. Increasingly, as I grow older, I experience the impurity of my body and the problems that come with that.

We tend to think of our body as somehow belonging to us. For example, as long as I am using this microphone I can refer to it as mine, but when I don't need it, it is not mine anymore. It is only at this moment that it is mine. If I think about my body in the same way, does it actually belong to me? Well, when you think about it, right now this physical body doesn't really belong to me. If I thought of this body as mine, I would be engaging in self-indulgence, thinking, "This is my body and I feel wonderful!" It actually belongs to whoever is using it as a tool in their practice. We are just sharing this body as a tool.

In Taiwan, our recent annual member's conference was attended by thousands of people. A guest remarked to me, "Shifu, you are so lucky to have so many disciples!" I said, "There is a Chinese saying that a good horse will never lack riders. So I'm just in this situation where a lot of people use me as a tool for their practice." When my master's master was in his seventies and still in very good health, I told him, "Grandmaster, I hope you live to be at least 120." He said, "Do I owe that much to you people?"

To lessen our vexation, we can at least tell ourselves that our body really belongs to everybody to be used as a tool. If we can't really be useful that way, at least we can remind ourselves that our body does not really belong to us. If you can do this, you will be less concerned about yourself and be willing to share yourself with others.

I once told someone, "You are truly a very fortunate man. Your parents are still healthy and alive, your children are well behaved, and your wife is so nice. You are indeed very fortunate to enjoy such great merit."

He responded, "Yes, I am indeed very fortunate. However, I am really my parents' crutches, my kids' playmate, and my wife's servant."

People who can really feel that they belong to their family and not to themselves are indeed fortunate and wise. Others may think, "My wife and children, they belong to me, and as for my parents, what they leave behind will belong to me." Someone like this will have a lot of vexation.

Mindfulness of Sensations

Most of the time, we are indifferent or at least neutral to the sensations we experience. At other times we react with feelings of pleasure or displeasure, happiness or unhappiness. Sensations we don't like make us uncomfortable, but even pleasant experiences disappear quickly, and this too causes discomfort if we crave more. So in addition to the impurity of the body, we contemplate how we use the senses to experience our body and the world.

For example, the sensations of pleasure and pain are actually very subjective and very relative. One person may say that work is painful whereas idleness is pleasant. They work hard and complain of fatigue and frustration: "What is the point of all this?" But for people striving to realize their vision, the harder they work the more energized they feel, and the greater the sense of accomplishment.

What constitutes suffering depends on one's attitude and point of view. For example, most people think that poverty, sickness, and old age are all forms of suffering. However, one can experience these things without necessarily suffering. Some sick people do not feel suffering. Some might even say, "This sickness is a blessing because through it I encountered the Dharma." Does this person experience pain? Probably, but pain is not necessarily the same as suffering. Pain is a physical experience, but suffering is an emotional response to what one feels physically. Even while experiencing your own pain, you should help other sentient beings that are having even greater troubles. When you can use your own discomfort to comfort others, you will suffer less.

The Buddhist sutras tell of bodhisattvas who vow to go to hell if necessary in order to deliver sentient beings. There they would encounter the discomfort and pain of hell without experiencing emotional suffering. The reason is that they are protected by their vow to help sentient beings. For these bodhisattvas, being in hell is no different from being in the Pure Land. That is not to say that hell is the same as the Pure Land, but since these bodhisattvas are not in hell to be punished, they experience no suffering. The point is that our responses to sensations are intimately related to what is in our mind. After all, it is because of our mind that we are able to experience sensations.

Mindfulness of the Mind

We speak of the mind and imagine it to be some kind of entity. Sometimes the mind seems very abstract, but in Chinese philosophy the mind is considered an organ of the heart, and the mind refers to all the thoughts that are in one's heart. A constant flow of thoughts passes through the mind. Thought after thought, they constantly change, each new one different from the previous. Even though it seems to us that there is a "self" behind these thoughts, if our thoughts are constantly changing, how can there be a permanent thing called the "self"?

When this constant flow of thoughts stops, it is possible for wisdom and compassion to arise. But when the mind is not stable, it knows only vexation and suffering. One moment we can be very good-hearted and the next moment very mean. This is because when the mind is not calm there is suffering, and there is neither wisdom nor compassion. And when the mind is neither all good nor all bad, one is confused.

It *is* possible to improve your mind to the point where you have fewer vexations. When you are unhappy, tell yourself the feeling is not only impermanent, but it is also possible for you to change things for the better. Tell yourself there is nothing inherent about suffering, and that you are suffering because of the way you view and respond to things. There is a Chinese saying, "If you step back and look at the situation in a different way, you will be able to see open skies and the vast ocean." Why plunge forward into more suffering when you can step back and see the situation in a better light? However, when experiencing very heavy vexation, ask yourself, "Who is giving rise to these vexations?" But do not come up with answers like, "Oh, it's my wife, my husband, my boss, and so on who is giving me all this vexation." Truly, these vexations result from one's own mind. When you realize that, you will know that it is not necessary to give rise to all these vexations.

Mindfulness of Dharmas

To truly realize that suffering originates in our own mind, we need to contemplate the selflessness of dharmas. All dharmas are phenomena, but we should distinguish between the material dharmas in the environment and the dharmas in the mind—thoughts, ideas, symbols, and feelings. Without the physical body, the functions of the mind cannot manifest. The coming together of material dharmas (including the body) and mental dharmas (thoughts) results in the notion of a separate "self." That self, coming together from constantly changing dharmas, must also be impermanent. Therefore we can ask ourselves just who it is that is giving rise to suffering. If one's mind is constantly changing and one's body is also constantly changing, and if the self is the result of the coming together of constantly changing phenomena, then who am I? What is there in this mix that is "me"? If we can understand there is no enduring "I," then it is possible to understand emptiness and realize wisdom.

There are two steps we can take to achieve this. First, instead of thinking of our body and mind as our self, we can think of them as tools to help sentient beings accomplish liberation. At home, our body and mind can be used by everyone in the family; in the wider society, it can be shared by everyone. That way, there will not remain any idea of "This is me," and "This belongs to me." The second step is to contemplate that all phenomena—body, mind, and environment—are constantly changing. There is nothing permanent there. Similarly, as regards the idea of a self that results from the confluence of body, mind, and environment, since all these conditioning factors have no inherent existence, there can also be no inherently existing self. If one can understand this, one will be able to realize emptiness and attain wisdom. However, it is important to understand that you can't just jump into wisdom and emptiness—one needs to start with understanding the impermanence of the self.

EIGHT CONCENTRATION

Why is Right Concentration the last of the noble paths, when in fact from the very beginning we practice concentration with the Four Foundations of Mindfulness? Then in the Four Steps to Magical Powers, we also cultivate concentration. When one has successfully cultivated one-pointed samadhi, where there are no extraneous thoughts, one's mind will not be disturbed by what happens in one's mind, body, or environment. In one-pointed samadhi the individual may experience levels of bliss but if there is still a sense of self, it is not the samadhi of Right Concentration. The difference is that one-pointed samadhi is worldly samadhi, whereas Right Concentration, or in Sanskrit, *samyak-samadhi*, is the samadhi of liberation. Samyak-samadhi is also called the noble samadhi, the true samadhi, the supreme samadhi. Why all these names? Because samyak-samadhi transcends all worldly samadhis. Worldly samadhi stops the mind on one point, while samyak-samadhi transcends that.

An ordinary mind that does not fluctuate greatly in daily life can be said to have some level of samadhi power. But if one seriously cultivates samadhi, we are then speaking in terms of the four dhyana levels and the eight samadhis. Buddhadharma sees the world of samsara as containing three realms—the desire realm, the form realm, and the formless realm. The desire realm has nothing to do with any of the dhyana levels, but in the realm of form one cultivates the four dhyanas: leaving behind unwholesomeness for joy, leaving behind discursive thinking as joy continues, the arising of feelings of well-being combined with the lessening of joy, leaving behind joy for evenness and clarity of mind. The formless realm involves the dhyanas of infinite space, infinite consciousness, only perfect stillness, and neither cognition nor noncognition. Together the dhyanas in the form realm and the dhyanas in the formless realm make up the eight levels of worldly samadhi. The ninth level is the unworldly samadhi of perfect enlightenment.

How do these samadhis relate to the ordinary world? Beings in the desire realm attach to and crave sensual pleasures. This desire extends to the quest for comfort, security, and possessions. As a result one attaches to and identifies with these desires and possessions. This typifies beings in the realm of desire. In the realm of form, someone in samadhi is released from the burdens of body and environment, and feels such joy and happiness that it is easy to become very attached to those feelings. This is also true when experiencing the samadhis of the formless realm. So in the realm of desire, one is attached to the pleasures of the sensual world, and in the form and formless realms, one is attached to the bliss of samadhi. Because they all involve attachment and desires, all these states are called worldly samadhi.

I often remind students to adopt a joyful attitude during retreat. But on retreat you are meditating all day, you are not allowed to talk, the food is very simple, and the sleeping arrangements are not that good. Under these circumstances, how can one be joyful? People who have never been to retreat have difficulty understanding this. In fact, some think that people who go on retreats are weird. Interestingly, many retreat participants keep coming back; for them Chan retreat is vacation, and they come with a joyful attitude. The peace and calm, and the release from the burdens of daily life are reasons they continue returning. I encourage those who have not been to a Chan retreat to give it a try. Some may have been to retreat, but feel ambivalent about going again. They are comfortable with their life as it is and don't want to change it too much; on the other hand, they also recognize the benefits one can gain on retreat. So they feel these conflicts. If you put aside a period of time every day to practice, you will find your mind becoming more stable, and you will find more peace and harmony within yourself. But you can enjoy even greater benefits if you set aside a longer period of time every year to practice. Going on retreat is a good way to do this.

As we have said, Buddhadharma consists of the three disciplines of precepts, samadhi, and wisdom. However, in the Noble Eightfold Path, concentration is the ultimate path because it leads to the deepest samadhi of all, the world-transcending samadhi of liberation. One who attaches to the worldly samadhis is still in the worldly realm. When one returns from the bliss of worldly samadhi, one is no different from any ordinary being with vexations and attachments. So one must understand that worldly samadhi is not the ultimate samadhi; one needs to transcend one's attachments to the pleasure of the material world as well as to the bliss of worldly samadhi. When one is finally able to do so, one can give rise to the wisdom without outflows, the wisdom that is without self. What is the wisdom without outflows? It is the wisdom in which one does not give rise to vexation and suffering. So long as one can continue to manifest this wisdom, one is liberated.

Buddhadharma speaks of the four fruition stages in the liberation of an arhat. At the first fruition, the arhat has an initial taste of liberation, while in the second and third fruitions the realization gets deeper. It is only at the fourth fruition level, where one is constantly in a liberated state, that one manifests wisdom and samadhi simultaneously.

Worldly samadhi is entered through sitting meditation. When this samadhi is deep and the mind and body are not moving at all, there are no unwholesome thoughts or behavior, and no vexations. So long as one continues in samadhi, one enjoys a great sense of freedom. Nevertheless, no matter how deep any worldly samadhi, it will inevitably end, as will the sense of freedom that goes with it. On the other hand, one who attains world-transcending samadhi will enjoy the sense of freedom and ease even when not meditating. While engaging in all the activities of daily life, one continues to be undisturbed by the environment. You are truly liberated when you can experience that at all times. Therefore, if one wants to cultivate samadhi, one should cultivate the samyak-samadhi of the Noble Eightfold Path.

The Wisdom of No-Self

For forty-five years after his enlightenment, the Buddha traveled around India teaching and delivering sentient beings. During this time he was not constantly sitting in meditation and enjoying worldly samadhi. As a completely liberated person, the Buddha was in samadhi at all times. Similarly, his disciples who were arhats and bodhisattvas also lived ordinary lives. Like the Buddha, they did not experience suffering while living amid the human world because they had already realized samyak-samadhi.

You may think that because you are not yet an arhat or a buddha, all this has nothing to do with you. That would be a mistake. In Mahayana Buddhism, especially in Chan, the emphasis is on cultivating samadhi simultaneously with the wisdom of no-outflows, and to use that in daily life. As you encounter problems in body, mind, or the environment, you can practice not being affected by them and not giving rise to suffering and vexation. Even without being an arhat or bodhisattva, one who practices this way will derive immediate and great benefits.

How does one practice so as not to be afflicted by life's inevitable problems? A woman I know discovered that she had a large tumor. Even as she consulted doctors to diagnose the problem, the tumor was growing. But this woman remembered hearing me say that the best time to practice was when you have a very serious illness. You turn your illness over to the doctors and you give your life to the bodhisattvas. After that you have nothing to do but practice. During this whole crisis she was very calm, while her family was devastated. What this woman did was apply the wisdom of no-self. Though one has not realized the wisdom of no-self, one can still use the wisdom of no-self taught by the Buddha. That is what she did, and in a sense she had the power of samadhi.

Therefore when you are in a crisis that you cannot avoid, please remind yourself that whatever the problem, it is not *you*. Your mind will be more stable and calm, and you will give rise to less suffering. But if you try to escape or reject your problems, you will suffer a great deal more. In the journey of life there will be many obstacles, crises, and problems you cannot completely eliminate. But it is possible to survive them peacefully and safely by using the wisdom of Buddhadharma. When you do that, you are in fact practicing Right

Concentration. Chan teaches that samadhi and wisdom are not separate from daily life. This is the meaning of wisdom and samadhi arising simultaneously.

The fourth noble truth tells us that the way out of suffering is through the Noble Eightfold Path. Therefore one can also say that unless one practices the Noble Eightfold Path, the Four Noble Truths have no meaning. As a teaching about how to depart from suffering, the Four Noble Truths also encompass the Twelve Links of Conditioned Arising, the nidanas, which are a description of samsaric suffering.

What are the nidanas? They are the twelve causal links that everyone experiences in each lifetime. The Twelve Links explain how and why sentient beings transmigrate through uncountable lifetimes until they experience liberation. The Noble Eightfold Path is precisely the means for accomplishing liberation while remaining fully engaged on the bodhisattva path of helping sentient beings. Although it is basic Buddhism, the Noble Eightfold Path is also an essential practice in the Mahayana ideal.

In theory, the Thirty-seven Aids to Enlightenment are a sequence of gradual practices leading to liberation in the Noble Eightfold Path. In this view, one goes from one practice to the next in each category, ultimately completing all thirty-seven practices. However, in actual practice this would not necessarily be the case. If one rigorously and diligently practices any of the seven categories and focuses one's efforts on that practice, then that can take one all the way to liberation. For example, if you focus on the Four Foundations of Mindfulness, delving deeply into them, you can surely attain liberation. Or if you choose to focus on Right Concentration, that can also carry you all the way to liberation. The teachings of the Thirty-seven Aids seem complex, involving many steps, stages, and levels. But when you engage in the practice, all you need is to delve deeply into one method and stay with it until it takes you to liberation. It is not that complicated and actually quite simple.

If you do not entirely understand the teachings of the Noble Eightfold Path, do not be too concerned. What is important is to remember that the Noble Eightfold Path is the wisdom that Shakyamuni Buddha bequeathed to all of us. Its purpose is to help human beings solve the two main problems in life, namely living and dying. In life we inevitably encounter problems and obstacles arising from our body, from our mind, from society, and from nature. The result is that we experience pain, suffering, and unhappiness. The Buddhadharma of the Noble Eightfold Path helps us to deal with these difficulties by following the Middle Way. In this manner we will not give rise to as much vexation and suffering, and we will feel more at ease with life. We will have a better chance to experience true happiness and joy.

The Buddha's wisdom also helps us with the inevitability of death. Depending on one's merit and karma, one may encounter few or many difficulties in life. But however much merit one is born with or accumulates, no one will escape death. When we accept and follow the teachings of the Noble Eightfold Path, we will not feel as terrified and helpless when we arrive at the final stage of our life. We will know that the Noble Eightfold Path will ultimately guide us toward liberation from vexation and suffering.

Editor's Afterword

AFTER READING THIS BOOK, readers for whom the Thirty-seven Aids to Enlightenment are new teachings may feel awe and wonderment. However, with practitioners for whom the landscape of the Thirty-seven Aids is already familiar, their feelings may also be one of awe and wonderment. If this were the case, why would a newcomer to these teachings respond similarly to one who has traversed much of the Path? It may be because no matter where one is in the Path, the Thirty-seven Aids will always appear as new and inexhaustible. For the beginner, the issue is to find an entry point to the practices; for the seasoned practitioner, there are multiple points of entry. But if approached with an open and sincere mind, is it possible to perceive the bodhipakshika any other way?

In the *Mahaparinirvana Sutra,* the Buddha addresses his audience as "bhikkhus." Clearly, he was talking to ordained monastics, and presumably all had at least begun, or even realized the path of the arhat. In admonishing them to diligently practice the bodhipakshika, the Buddha was most likely not telling them anything they had not heard before. In fact, he says, "These, bhikkhus, are the teachings of which I have direct knowledge, *which I have made known to you . . .*" (emphasis mine). Rather, what they were hearing from the Buddha was more in the nature of a reminder, a summing up, a caution, a final request.

Most likely, all the monastics in the audience had their own unique experience of the Thirty-seven Aids. And following the admonition, each one had an opportunity to respond to the Buddha's request in their own way, influenced by vows, diligence, intention, attention, concentration, and skillful means in practice. Except for those like Mahakashyapa, who was by then liberated, there must have also been awe and wonderment at this final teaching.

If the Buddha thought that the Thirty-seven Aids were absolutely clear and settled in everyone's mind, why would he bother to admonish them about it near his death? It is reasonable to infer that the Buddha knew that among the community, there was still some doubt, some lack of clarity, and even uncertainty of purpose. It was another demonstration of the Buddha's great compassion that, even as he approached death, he made this request for them to reflect on. It was his final gift, in the form of a transmission of the teachings. And it is no less a gift to us.

Among those present, the one whose situation was most poignant was Ananda, the Buddha's beloved cousin, and the one to whom above all the Buddha entrusted the memory of his teachings. While preparing for his own demise, the Buddha had appealed to Ananda to take him on various pilgrimages, and to gather the monks so that they could hear his last sermon. We also know from the records that while Ananda had a glimpse of enlightenment, he was not yet fully liberated. Thus, even while performing missions for the Buddha that required mindfulness and compassion, Ananda had doubts about his own attainments.

After the Buddha's nirvana, Ananda pleaded to Mahakashyapa, the Buddha's successor, for help in achieving full liberation. Again and again, Mahakashyapa declined to help. Finally, Ananda realized that he must rely on his own efforts—starting with leaving behind his doubts—and he attained liberation through his own efforts.

It would not be too far-fetched for those not yet liberated to see in Ananda a reflection of their own situation, but in a smaller context. If even Ananda, who had the direct mentoring of a completely enlightened Buddha, could not ascend the heights while the Blessed One still lived, then that signals to us the enormity of the task ahead. At the same time, it also reveals to us the Buddha's infinite patience and loving-kindness to entrust Ananda with his personal security and the future of the Dharma.

So after the Buddha's nirvana, Ananda's situation was something of a paradox, requiring him to put aside his doubts while continuing to help sentient beings. At the same time, it was an opportunity to apply the skillful means that would take him to eventual liberation. If readers of this book can see Ananda's situation as in some ways a paradigm for their own practice—whether lay or monastic—that may be a step toward dispelling some wonderment while leaving awe intact. And with good causes and conditions, they may meet along the way some "learned friends" and able mentors.

However, we should not forget the concluding words of the Buddha's admonishment: "These [teachings] you should thoroughly learn, cultivate, develop, and frequently practice, that the life of purity may be established and may long endure, for the welfare and happiness of the multitude, out of compassion for the world, for the benefit, well-being, and happiness of gods and men."

The Thirty-seven Aids to Enlightenment
(Bodhi pakshika Dharma)

(Note: Parenthesized terms are in Sanskrit.)

THE FOUR FOUNDATIONS OF MINDFULNESS
(SMRITI-UPASTHANA)

Mindfulness of the body (*kaya-nupassana*)
Mindfulness of sensations (*vedana-nupassana*)
Mindfulness of the mind (*citta-nupassana*)
Mindfulness of dharmas (*dharma-nupassana*)

THE FOUR PROPER EXERTIONS (SAMYAK-PRAHANANI)

To keep unwholesome states not yet arisen from arising
    (*anuppadaya*)
To cease unwholesome states already arisen (*pahanaya*)
To give rise to wholesome states not yet arisen (*uppadaya*)
To continue wholesome states already arisen (*thitiya*)

THE FOUR STEPS TO MAGICAL POWERS (RIDDHIPADA)

Concentration of desire (*chanda*)
Concentration of exertion (*virya*)
Concentration of mind (*chitta*)
Concentration of inquiry (*mimamsa*)

THE FIVE ROOTS (INDRIYA)

Faith (*shraddha*)
Diligence (*virya*)
Mindfulness (*smriti*)
Concentration (*samadhi*)
Wisdom (*prajna*)

THE FIVE POWERS (BALA)

Faith (*shraddha*)
Diligence (*virya*)
Mindfulness (*smriti*)
Concentration (*samadhi*)
Wisdom (*prajna*)

THE SEVEN FACTORS OF ENLIGHTENMENT (SAPTA-BODHYANGA)

Mindfulness (*smriti*)
Discernment (*dharmavicaya*)
Diligence (*virya*)
Joy (*priti*)
Lightness-and-ease (*prasrabdhi*)

Concentration (*samadhi*)
Equanimity (*upeksha*)

THE NOBLE EIGHTFOLD PATH
(ARYA ASHTANGIKA-MARGA)

Right View (*samyak-dristhi*)
Right Intention (*samyak-samkalpa*)
Right Speech (*samyak-vach*)
Right Action (*samyak-karmanta*)
Right Livelihood (*samyak-ajiva*)
Right Effort (*samyak-vyayama*)
Right Mindfulness (*samyak-smriti*)
Right Concentration (*samyak-samadhi*)

Glossary

Abhidharma: (Skt.) The Abhidharma is the third part of the Tripitaka, or "three baskets" that make up the Buddhist canon: the Vinaya (codes of conduct), the Sutras (discourses of the Buddha), and the Abhidharma (analysis of phenomena and treatises). The treatises, or shastras, of the Abhidharma are mainly additions to the canon made by the later Mahayana scholars.

Agamas: (Skt.) In Buddhism, a generic term referring to the Sanskrit sutras later translated into Chinese. These form the second part of the Tripitaka.

Amitabha: The buddha of the Western Paradise (the Pure Land) who symbolizes mercy and wisdom. Through Amitabha Buddha's vow, any person who sincerely invokes his name and expresses the wish to be born in the Pure Land will be reborn there. The Pure Land practice of reciting Amitabha's name is one of the most accessible and simple forms of Buddhism. See also **Pure Land.**

Arhat: (Skt., lit., "worthy one") In Buddhism the arhat is one who has completed the course of practice and has attained liberation in nirvana. As such, the arhat is no longer subject to rebirth. Some of the hallmarks of the arhat state are overcoming all doubt about the Dharma and putting aside all desires and attachments. There are four fruition levels in the course of becoming an arhat: (1) stream-enterer—one who has eradicated wrong views but is not entirely free of the "three poisons" of desire, anger, and ignorance; (2) once-returner—one in whom the defilements are only slightly present and who will be reborn only once more; (3) never-returner—one who is free from the five fetters of ego, doubt, ritual, sensuality, and envy, and will not be reborn;

(4) arhat—one who has attained nirvana, the state of no more learning, with all defilements extinguished, and is liberated from rebirth.

Avalokiteshvara: (Skt., lit., "the Lord who looks down [on the world of suffering]") Avalokiteshvara is the bodhisattva who embodies the compassion of the buddhas, who listens and responds to the supplications of sentient beings who ask for his help. In Chinese Buddhism Avalokiteshvara is known as Guanyin (J., Kannon), and is sometimes, but not always, regarded as having a feminine persona. In Tibetan Buddhism, Avalokiteshvara has a male aspect as Chenrezig, and a female aspect as Tara. In Korean Buddhism, Avalokiteshvara is known as Kwan Um.

Bhikkhu: (Pali) In Theravada Buddhism, a monk. The Sanskrit term is *bhikshu,* used in Mahayana traditions. For nuns, the term is *bhikkhuni* in Pali, *bhikshuni* in Sanskrit.

Bodhi-mind: "The mind of wisdom." A central idea in Mahayana Buddhism, its meaning varies depending on the context: (1) the initial arousal of the aspiration to attain buddhahood while helping sentient beings, this being the first step in establishing oneself on the bodhisattva path; (2) the state of mind upon genuinely awakening to the emptiness of the self, this also being an experience of enlightenment; and (3) the state of mind when acting selflessly in accordance with one's bodhisattva vows.

Bodhisattva: (Skt., lit., "awakened being") Considered the role model in the Mahayana tradition, a bodhisattva vows to postpone one's own attainment of buddhahood for the sake of helping sentient beings. See also **Bodhi-mind.**

Caodong: (J., Soto) Along with the Linji (J., Rinzai) sect, the Caodong is one of the two major surviving sects of Chan and Zen Buddhism. Like the Linji sect, Caodong espouses sudden enlightenment but with greater emphasis on the practice of Silent Illumination (*shikantaza* in Japanese), as opposed to the methods of gong'an (J., koan) and huatou (J., *wato*). See also **Huatou, Silent Illumination.**

Chan: See **Dhyana.**

Conditioned Arising: Also known as dependent origination, conditioned arising is the Buddhist doctrine that all phenomena (dharmas) come into existence and cease to exist as a result of a myriad of causes and conditions. No thing exists or occurs unless conditions permit it; phenomena exist interdependently, depending on other phenomena for their arising and cessation.

Dharma/dharma: (Skt., lit., "holding"; Pali, *dhamma*) The word *dharma* has two important senses in Buddhism. One refers to the body of teachings of Buddhism as taught by the Buddha. In this sense, the word is also synonymous with Buddhadharma. Dharma also refers to any object or phenomenon arising out of causes and conditions, including external as well as mental ones. As a convention often used in English, *Dharma* (with an uppercase *D*) refers to the teachings of the Buddha, while *dharma* (with a lowercase *d*) refers to any physical or mental phenomenon. See also **Three Jewels.**

Dhyana: (Skt.) Generically, *dhyana* refers to any of the various methods of concentrative absorption (meditation) that are used in Buddhism. The specific meanings of dhyana refer to the levels of absorption in the form and formless realms. Together, the four dhyanas of the form realm and the four dhyanas of the formless realm comprise the eight levels of worldly samadhi. Worldly samadhis are those in which, however refined, there are still mental attachments. A ninth level of samadhi, the unworldly, represents complete enlightenment. In practice, the progressive levels of dhyana of the form realm are of greatest interest. They are: (1) relinquishing of unwholesome factors and the appearance of bliss; (2) bliss continues while relinquishing discursive thinking; (3) abatement of bliss as feelings of well-being arise; (4) relinquishing joy for equanimity and clarity of mind. The dhyanas of the formless realm are (1) infinite spaciousness, (2) infinite consciousness, (3) nothing except perfect stillness, (4) neither thought nor no-thought. "Chan" is the Chinese transliteration of *dhyana*, and "Zen" is the Japanese transliteration of "Chan." See also **Samadhi.**

Eight Worldly Samadhis: See **Samadhi.**

Five Aggregates: See **Skandhas.**

Five Desires: The five sensual pleasures associated with the five senses: form, sound, aroma, taste, and touch.

Five Hindrances: The five hindrances are negative qualities that hinder progress toward achieving samadhi and enlightenment. They are desire, anger, sloth, restlessness, and doubt. The influence of the five hindrances can be offset by cultivating the five wholesome faculties. See also **Five Wholesome Faculties.**

Five Methods of Stilling the Mind: The Five Methods of Stilling the Mind are (1) contemplating the breath, (2) contemplating the impurity of the body, (3) contemplating loving-kindness, (4) contemplating causes and conditions, and (5) depending on the tradition, the fifth may be contemplating the limits of phenomena or contemplating the name of a buddha.

Five Powers: The fifth in the seven groups of practices that make up the Thirty-seven Aids to Enlightenment, the Five Powers (Skt., bala) are faith, diligence, mindfulness, concentration, and wisdom. These five factors are the counterparts of the fourth group, the Five Roots (Skt., indriya), and build on the virtues attained by practicing the Five Roots. Practicing the Five Roots gives rise to the correspondingly named Five Powers. The Five Powers in turn enhance one's ability to cultivate wisdom and compassion. Thus, progressing through the Five Roots and Five Powers, one continues with virtue and vigor on the path to enlightenment. See also **Five Roots.**

Five Precepts: The five precepts of Buddhism are the basic guidelines for moral behavior: not to kill, not to steal, not to engage in sexual misconduct, not to speak falsehoods, and not to indulge in intoxicants. The vows to uphold the precepts are normally taken when one takes refuge in the Three Jewels of Buddhism: the Buddha, the Dharma, and the Sangha. For monastics there are additional precepts, taken with the ordination vows. See also **Three Jewels.**

Five Roots: The fourth in the seven groups of practices that make up the Thirty-seven Aids to Enlightenment, the Five Roots (Skt., indriya) are virtues that are cultivated through the practice of samadhi (meditative concentration). They are faith, diligence, mindfulness, concentration, and wisdom. Cultivating the Five Roots means making further progress along the path established by the earlier practices, namely, the Four Foundations of Mindfulness, the Four Proper Exertions, and the Four Steps to Magical Powers. Practicing the Five Roots should lead to giving rise to the Five Powers and their corresponding factors. See also **Five Powers.**

Five Wholesome Faculties: The five wholesome faculties are the so-called virtuous roots of faith, diligence, mindfulness, concentration, and wisdom, which when cultivated through practice, give rise to the five corresponding so-called powers of faith, diligence, mindfulness, concentration, and wisdom. Together they make up the Five Roots and Five Powers, the fourth and fifth group of practices in the Thirty-seven Aids to Enlightenment. See also **Five Hindrances.**

Five Worldly Desires: Wealth, sex, fame, food, sleep.

Four Dhyanas: See **Dhyana.**

Four Enhanced Phenomena: Virtuous qualities that may grow out of diligent practice: (1) warmth, (2) summit, (3) forbearance, and (4) supreme in the world. In warmth the mind's harshness recedes; in summit one's mind has ascended to the dhyana peak; in forbearance one no longer harms oneself or others; in supreme in the world one transcends worldliness and approaches liberation.

Glossary

Four Foundations of Mindfulness: The Four Foundations of Mindfulness are mindfulness of the body, mindfulness of sensations, mindfulness of mind, and mindfulness of phenomena (dharmas). These mindfulness factors are cultivated through contemplation (meditative concentration) in order to achieve samadhi, the one-pointed state of mind in which there are few if any thoughts. This state of mind is often equated with bliss.

Four Noble Truths: The first sermon given by the Buddha after his enlightenment was on the Four Noble Truths: (1) the truth of the existence of suffering, (2) the truth that the origin of suffering is ignorance, (3) the truth that suffering can be ceased, and (4) the truth that cessation of suffering comes through following the Noble Eightfold Path, which consists of Right View, Right Intention, Right Speech, Right Action, Right Livelihood, Right Effort, Right Mindfulness, and Right Concentration.

Four Steps to Magical Power: The Four Steps to Magical Power (Skt., riddhipada) make up the third group of practices in the Thirty-seven Aids to Enlightenment. In terms of sequence, they follow the Four Foundations of Mindfulness and the Four Proper Exertions. The four steps are (1) exerting one's desire to practice the methods of dhyana, (2) applying diligence to one's efforts, (3) bringing one's mind to focus totally on practicing dhyana, and (4) using wisdom to keep one's mind in the proper state for practice. The purpose of the Four Steps to Magical Power is also to overcome hindrances to practice.

Hinayana: (Skt., lit., "lesser vehicle") A term the later Mahayana ("greater vehicle") School of Buddhism applied to the early schools of Buddhism. The term "Hinayana" was meant to distinguish the emphasis on self-liberation of early Buddhism from the Mahayana emphasis on postponing self-liberation for the sake of sentient beings. The early schools, including that of the Theravada, did not use the term "Hinayana" to describe their own tradition. See also **Mahayana.**

Huatou: (Chin., lit., "head of a thought") The Chan method in which a practitioner investigates a question, such as "What is my original face before birth and death?" By intensively seeking the answer to the huatou, the mind of the practitioner may develop a "great ball of doubt," and the resolution of this may result in insight or awakening.

Karma: (Skt., lit., "action, deed") In Buddhism, karma is the law of cause and effect which holds that all our actions, words, and thoughts have consequences that manifest as retribution, from causes laid down in previous lives, in the present life, and extending to future lives. The most important factor in determining the nature and quality of retribution is intention. Where there is no intention, the karmic burden can be very light to nonexistent. When intention is strong, the karmic burden will be strong. Correspondingly, wholesome and virtuous actions, words, and thoughts yield positive retribution. So the overall impact of karmic accumulation is a balancing of all our actions, words, and thoughts, wholesome as well as unwholesome.

Mahayana: (Skt., lit., "great vehicle") The name Mahayana was used by the later Sanskrit-based schools of Buddhism to describe their own tradition, as distinct from the earlier schools of Buddhism, which they called Hinayana ("lesser vehicle"). In the eyes of the Mahayanists, the so-called Hinayana schools' emphasis on personal liberation did not go far enough. Instead, the Mahayana view is that the purpose of the path was primarily to deliver sentient beings, and only then should one work for personal liberation. The early schools of Buddhism did not accept the term "Hinayana" to describe their own tradition. Today early Buddhism is mostly represented by the Theravada tradition. See also **Hinayana.**

Mind-Only School: See **Yogachara.**

Nagarjuna: One of the most important Indian scholars and philosophers (ca. 150–250 C.E.) associated with the Mahayana tradition of Buddhism. Nagarjuna was considered one of the great exponents of the Buddhist concept of emptiness in later Buddhism. His most notable achievement was his explication of the philosophy of the *Madhyamaka,* or Middle Way, in which one neither posits the reality of existence nor denies the reality of existence. His most important treatise was the *Mulamadhyamaka-karika* (Treatise on the Middle Way).

Nidanas: (Skt.) Also known as the Twelve Links of Conditioned Arising, as well as the Twelve Links of Dependent Origination, the nidanas are ignorance, action, consciousness, name-and-form, the six sense faculties, contact, sensation, desire, clinging, becoming, birth, and aging-and-dying.

Nikaya: (Skt., Pali, lit., "corpus," "body") Collectively, the Buddhist canon associated with early Buddhism, written in the Pali dialect. The term "Nikaya Buddhism" does not designate a formal school, but simply refers to the early Buddhism associated with the Nikaya canon.

Nirvana: (Skt., lit., "extinction") A state of existence in which a being is no longer subject to samsara, the cycle of birth and death. In this state one has extinguished all desires and attachments to worldly samsaric existence, and thus will not be destined for rebirth. From the point of view of the stages of fruition in practice, nirvana is the ultimate state where one has nothing more to learn. According to Mahayana teachings, all buddhas have attained nirvana, but not all who attain nirvana have attained full buddhahood. See also **Parinirvana, Samsara.**

Noble Eightfold Path: The Noble Eightfold Path consists of Right View, Right Intention, Right Speech, Right Action, Right Livelihood, Right Effort, Right Mindfulness, and Right Concentration.

No-self: (Skt., *anatman*) A central idea in Buddhism that stipulates that what is ordinarily considered a person is essentially an aggregate of phenomenal factors called the five skandhas. The five skandhas operating together create the illusion in sentient beings of being a separate, independently existing "self." This belief in self is the source of suffering. Therefore, the course of practice in Buddhism is for the purpose of realizing the illusory nature of "self." See also **Skandhas.**

Paramitas: (Skt., lit., "perfections") The Six Paramitas are virtues that a Buddhist practitioner should cultivate: generosity, morality, patience, diligence, meditation, and wisdom.

Parinirvana: (Skt.; Pali; *parinibbana*) Although sometimes used synonymously with the term "nirvana," *parinirvana* usually refers to the death and entrance into nirvana of one who attained complete liberation while still alive, as in the case of the Buddha. See also **Nirvana, Samsara.**

Precepts: See **Five Precepts, Three Disciplines.**

Pure Land: The Land of Supreme Bliss, or the Western Paradise, of Amitabha Buddha. Through Amitabha Buddha's vow, any person who sincerely invokes his name and expresses the wish to be born in the Pure Land will be reborn there. Traditionally, Pure Land practice consists of mindfully reciting the name of Amitabha Buddha. See also **Amitabha.**

Samadhi: (Skt., lit., "make firm") A state of meditative concentration in which one's mind is free from stray thoughts and vexations, though in shallower samadhi there still remains awareness of self. In Buddhist meditation practice, there are nine levels of samadhi. The first eight samadhis are called worldly samadhis because there are still attachments and desires. The first four samadhis are the dhyanas in the realm of form, and the next four samadhis are the dhyanas in the realm of no-form. Together they make the first eight samadhis. The ninth samadhi is the unworldly samadhi of enlightenment. In this state samadhi and wisdom are simultaneous. See also **Dhyana.**

Samsara: (Skt.) In Buddhism, the birth-and-death cycle of transmigration to which sentient beings are subject until they attain nirvana. See also **Triloka.**

Sangha: (Skt., lit., "assembly," "community") In Buddhism, the narrower meaning of *sangha* refers to the community of all ordained Buddhist monks and nuns, and also to the monastic members of a single monastery or temple. In a wider sense *sangha* refers to the community of all Buddhists, including laypeople. The Sangha is also one of the Three Jewels of Buddhism: namely. Buddha, Dharma, and Sangha. See also **Dharma, Three Jewels.**

SARS: (Severe Acute Respiratory Syndrome) An infectious viral disease that has broken out periodically, mostly in the Far East, and at times has approached epidemic status.

Seven Factors of Enlightenment: (Skt., sapta-bodhyanga) The Seven Factors of Enlightenment comprise the sixth of the seven groups of practices in the Thirty-seven Aids to Enlightenment. Together they identify seven practice factors that are conducive to enlightenment: mindfulness, discernment, diligence, joy, lightness-and-ease, concentration, and equanimity. Within the context of the Thirty-seven Aids to Enlightenment, the Seven Factors follow sequentially the groups of practices beginning with the Four Foundations of Mindfulness. However, within the Seven Factors themselves, the practices are also considered to be sequential beginning with mindfulness and ending with equanimity.

Shastra: In Buddhism, a scholarly treatise or analysis, most often based on one of the Buddha's sutras. See also **Sutra.**

Shifu: (Chin., also "Sifu") Honorific for a teacher with whom one is affiliated as a student. In other words, the term is used by a student in addressing their teacher.

Shikantaza: (J., lit., "just sitting") Japanese Zen practice that is very similar to Silent Illumination of Chinese Chan. See also **Silent Illumination.**

Shravaka: (Skt., lit., "one who hears") One who practices Buddhism in order to attain personal liberation in nirvana. In this sense the term is somewhat synonymous with "arhat." Another sense of shravaka is one of the original disciples who heard the Dharma directly from the Buddha.

Silent Illumination: Silent Illumination is a Chan method in which one focuses on the act of one's body sitting in meditation to the exclusion of all other thoughts, allowing the mind to settle into a silent state of illumined clarity. See also **Shikantaza.**

Skandhas (Skt., lit., "heaps," "aggregates") The five skandhas are the constituents of the sentient being's experience of the world. They are form, sensation, perception, volition, and consciousness. The first skandha, form, is the material component; the other four are mental in nature. Operating together, the five skandhas create the illusion of separate existence and the notion of self, or ego.

Soto: See **Caodong.**

Sutra: (Skt.) In Buddhism, a discourse usually spoken by the Buddha, as distinct from a shastra, which is a commentary on a sutra.

Tathagata: (Skt., lit., "thus come/thus gone") Generically, the term refers to an incarnated buddha, one who has appeared among sentient beings. However, when capitalized, the term is also one of several epithets of the historical Buddha, Shakyamuni.

Ten Virtues: The ten virtues are the wholesome aspects of daily life conduct for Buddhists. The virtues relating to action are not to kill, not to steal, and not to commit sexual misconduct. The virtues relating to speech are refraining from lying, refraining from slander, refraining from gossip, and refraining from divisive speech. The virtues relating to the mind are cutting off greed, cutting off hatred, and cutting off ignorance. The ten nonvirtues (sometimes called the ten evils) are the opposites of the ten virtues.

Three Disciplines: The three disciplines (or studies) of Buddhism consist of morality, concentration, and wisdom. The three categories are folded into the Noble Eightfold Path in the following way: Morality entails Right Speech, Right Action, and Right Livelihood. Concentration (meditation) entails Right Effort, Right Mindfulness, and Right Concentration. Wisdom entails Right View and Right Intention.

Three Jewels: The Three Jewels of Buddhism are the Buddha, the Dharma, and the Sangha. The Buddha is the primordial teacher of Buddhism, the Dharma is what he taught, and the Sangha is the community of believers and followers. See also **Dharma, Three Refuges.**

Three Kinds of Sensations: Relative to the practice of mindfulness of sensations, Buddhism speaks of three ways we respond to sensations: with pleasure, neutrally, and with pain. The practice of mindful awareness is to take note of our own responses to sensations—whether they be pleasurable, neutral, or painful—without overly attaching to or being repelled by them.

Three Kinds of Suffering: Buddhism speaks of three kinds, or aspects, of suffering: the suffering of suffering, the suffering of change, and pervasive suffering. The suffering of suffering is tangible suffering, such as when we cut a finger and feel pain. The suffering of change is more subtle; it is the suffering caused by the fact that things are impermanent and undergo change, most notably when we lose something we cherish. Pervasive suffering is the most subtle and derives from the nature of conditioned existence itself, the yearning for an absolute where there is none, and is therefore pervasive. This last kind of suffering is similar to existential angst.

Three Poisons: The three poisons (Skt., *kleshas*) are deep-rooted defilements of the mind that lead to unwholesome states and activities. The continued existence of the defilements become obstructions to bringing suffering to a cease, and perpetuates the cycle of rebirth. There are many variant translations of the three poisons, but very common are the following, respectively: greed or desire, hatred or aversion, and ignorance or delusion (Skt., *trishna, upadana, avidya*).

Three Realms: See **Triloka.**

Three Refuges: Taking the Three Refuges is the ceremony in which one declares one's faith in the Three Jewels: the Buddha, the Dharma, and the Sangha. The Buddha is the enlightened teacher, the Dharma consists of his teachings, and the Sangha is the community of monastics and laypeople who practice Buddhism.

Triloka: (Skt., lit., "three worlds") Samsara, the cycle of birth and death, consists of the three realms: the realm of desire, the realm of form, and the formless realm. The desire realm is made up of six planes of existence into which sentient beings may be reborn: *devas* (heavenly beings), *asuras* (jealous demigods), human beings, animals, *pretas* (hungry ghosts), and *narakas* (hell beings). Beings in the form realm have a subtle corporeal nature but have no desire for sexual contact or food. Sentient beings are reborn into this realm by practicing the four dhyanas of the form realm. Beings in the formless realm are pure spirits lacking corporeal nature and abide in the dhyana heavens. Sentient beings are reborn into this realm by practicing the dhyanas of the formless realm. See also **Dhyana.**

Tripitaka (Skt., lit. "three baskets") A generic term referring to the three groups ("baskets") of the Buddhist canon, the Vinaya (codes of conduct), the Sutras (discourses of the Buddha), and the Abhidharma (analysis of phenomena and treatises).

Twelve Links of Conditioned Arising: See **Nidanas.**

Vinaya: (Skt.) See **Tripitaka.**

Yogachara: (Skt., lit., "practice of yoga") One of the most important schools in the Indian Mahayana tradition, which began around the fourth century. The Indian philosophers most associated with the school are Asanga and

Vasubandhu. The fundamental idea of the Yogachara school is that all phenomena are manifestations of the activities of the mind with its eight levels of consciousness. This focus gave rise to the designation of the school as the Mind-Only or the Consciousness-Only school.

Zen: A major school of Mahayana Buddhism founded in Japan around the twelfth century with ancestral roots from Chinese Chan. The kinship between Chan and Zen runs deep, to the point where both traditions honor the same ancestral founders, beginning with the Indian monk Bodhidharma, who entered China around the sixth century. After taking root in Japan, Zen developed its own unique style and flavor while retaining the methods and philosophy of Chan. In fact, the two existing schools of Chinese Chan, the Linji and the Caodong, still have their counterparts in Japan as the Rinzai and Soto schools. The word "Zen" is derived from the word "Chan" just as "Chan" is derived from the Indian *dhyana*, meaning meditation. See also **Dhyana.**

Index

Abhidharma, 3–4, 21
action. *See* Right Action
agamas, 99
aids to enlightenment. *See* Thirty-
    seven Aids to Enlightenment
Amitabha Buddha, 12, 76
anger, 32
animals
    killing, 152–54
    suffering, 152–54
arhat, 35, 49, 50, 166, 167
    becoming an, 6, 39, 43, 46, 73, 78, 82,
        83, 85, 139, 166, 167
arising and perishing, 142–45. *See also*
        conditioned arising; samsara
asceticism, 130
attachment
    to body, 23, 66, 87–88, 159
    See also nonattachment
Avalokiteshvara, 12, 76
avidya, 138

birth-and-death cycle. *See* death;
    samsara
bliss, 16–17

bodhi-mind, 146–47
bodhipakshika/bodhipakkhiya
    defined, 1
    nature of, 2–3
    references in Abhidharma, 3–4
    role in enlightenment, 4–7
    spatial view of, 6
    temporal view of, 6–7
bodhisattva mind, arousing the,
    132–33
bodhisattva path, 46, 80
    Buddha's wisdom and, 118–19
    and delivering others before
        delivering oneself, 132–33
    dhyana and, 52, 54
    foundation, 55, 131
    vs. Hinayana path of the *shravaka*,
        86 (*see also* Hinayana
        Buddhism)
    liberation path and, 131
    Noble Eightfold Path and, 131
    virtuous roots and, 55, 71, 72
    See also liberation
bodhisattva practice of Six
        Paramitas, 36

Index

Index

turnings, three, 77–78
Twelve Links of Conditioned Arising, 137, 168

upeksha (equanimity), 98

vegetarianism, 153–54
vexations, 14, 30–31, 64, 162
view. *See* Right View
virtue
    cultivating, 5
    levels of, 71
    samadhi and, 5–6
virtues, ten, 28–29
virtuous roots, five, 55, 60, 75, 99–101
virya (concentration of exertion), 48, 49, 53

warmth, 46, 52
wholesome faculties, five, 33–34
wholesome vs. unwholesome
    behavior, 93–94, 148
    karma, 66, 79–81
    states, 29–31, 62–64, 93, 94
wisdom, 33, 34, 59, 72
    enhancing the roots of, 77–83
    of no-self, 166–69
    paths of, 135–48
    "people with wisdom," 100–101
    types of, 105
    vs. vexation, 90
    without outflows, 166, 167
    See also liberation: wisdom and

Yogachara (Mind-Only) school, 21

9 781590 307908